I SPOKE TO YOU WITH SILENCE

I SPOKE TO YOU
WITH SILENCE

Essays from Queer Mormons of Marginalized Genders

EDITED BY
KERRY SPENCER PRAY
AND
JENN LEE SMITH

THE UNIVERSITY OF UTAH PRESS
Salt Lake City

The Defiance House Man colophon is a registered trademark of
The University of Utah Press. It is based on a four-foot-tall Ancient
Puebloan pictograph (late PIII) near Glen Canyon, Utah.

ISBN: 978-1-64769-079-3 (paperback)
ISBN: 978-1-64769-080-9 (ebook)
Cataloging-in-Publication data for this title is available online
at the Library of Congress.

Cover design by Jessica Booth, based on an image by Nataly/stock.Adobe.com.

Errata and further information on this and other titles available
online at UofUpress.com

Printed and bound in the United States of America.

Dedicated to the memory of Berta Marquez

CONTENTS

PART III: ESSAYS ON SHAME, SUICIDE, AND THE CLOSET

PART IV: ESSAYS ON THE CHURCH

FOREWORD

Lisa Diamond

Although many Western religious traditions make a big deal about gender and sex, there are few faith traditions that have the particular preoccupation—and strict enforcement of rules—of the Mormon Church (also known as the Church of Jesus Christ of Latter-day Saints, commonly abbreviated LDS). This is why the essays in this volume are so powerful, absorbing, inspiring, and heartbreaking. So many different voices and experiences are represented and celebrated here, across the entire spectrum of sexual and gender diversity. Each voice is unique—although all of the authors have experienced marginalization by the LDS Church because of their sexuality and/or gender, the nuances of their experiences, and the paths that they followed as a result, are as individual as fingerprints. There is not *one* path through life as a sexually diverse or gender-diverse member of the church, *there are as many paths as there are people*, and this volume provides a much-needed window into these journeys.

I was not raised LDS myself; I am an agnostic cisgender lesbian (raised by a lapsed Baptist and an ardent atheist, and currently married to a Jewish woman), and I knew nothing about the church's teachings about gender and sexuality until I moved to Salt Lake City in 1999 to accept a faculty position at the University of Utah. Colleagues warned me and my partner about the church's retrograde views of sexuality and gender. Although many contemporary religious faiths (such as Catholicism, various Protestant traditions, and my wife's conservative Judaism) have become more accepting of sexual and gender diversity over the years, this has not been the case for the LDS Church. In fact, some would argue that the church has doubled down on its restrictive notions of sex and gender over the past decade, in direct response to larger social changes such as the legalization of same-gender marriage and the growing visibility of individuals whose gender identities and expressions do not align with their birth-assigned sex/gender. The church has made it abundantly clear that the *only* gender acknowledged by the church—and by Heavenly Father—is one's birth-assigned gender. Although they have publicly acknowledged that transgender and other gender-diverse individuals exist, they instruct such individuals *not* to pursue any form of medical or social transition if they want to remain members of the church. Similarly, the church claims to accept members with same-gender attractions, but only if they commit to *never acting* on those attractions, till their dying day.

Some have described these views as a "softening" of the church's stance on gender and sexuality, but it is difficult to see the "soft" part. Although the church now acknowledges the basic existence of sexually diverse and gender-diverse individuals, it makes crystal clear that these individuals are not lovable—not spiritually or personally worthy—as their true, authentic selves. Only by stifling and suppressing your selfhood, your thoughts, your feelings, your dreams, your emotions—can you remain part of the fold. Certainly, many members of the faith have come to adopt more affirming views of sexual and gender diversity on a personal level, but the gap between such affirmative views and the church's official teachings is profound.

Individuals who are unfamiliar with LDS culture (as I certainly was before 1999) often wonder why queer or trans individuals (and/or their family members) don't just leave the church. This was my simplistic thinking twenty years ago, when I first started meeting so many LDS individuals who had experienced so much pain at the hands of church leaders, bishops, ward members, and often their own families. If your church does not accept you, just leave. *Just leave*—not so easy, especially not in Utah, the cultural and spiritual heart of the faith. Walking away can mean disconnecting from your entire social support network—everyone you grew up with, everyone you trust, every safety net that you have. For some—especially those with children of their own—this price can be too steep. And even for individuals who *do* choose to leave, the effects of marginalization linger. Can you just "leave" the thoughts and teachings about gender and sexuality that have marked your passage all the way from primary school to college? Can you "forget" that women who engage in sexual activity are as worthless as a chewed-up piece of gum, that same-gender attractions are a "burden" that will hopefully be lifted in the Celestial Kingdom, that gender is eternal and cannot be modified or questioned, that masturbation is a horrible violation, that sexual imagery is as dangerous as illicit drugs, and that you have failed as a parent if your child never marries? In the same way that individuals cannot suddenly switch from driving on the right-hand side of the street to the left-hand side, they cannot easily undo years of socialization and indoctrination.

One of the strengths of this volume is that the stories speak to the diversity of LDS experiences—the church's teachings may be consistently exclusionary, but many *individual* members of the church strive for authentic inclusiveness and connection. I have witnessed this firsthand: During over twenty years of living and teaching in Utah, my wife and I have developed deep and abiding friendships with many current and former members of the church. We have attended their weddings (at least, the portions that we were permitted to) and they have attended ours. We have celebrated the births of their children and grandchildren. We have answered their questions when they discover that members of their own family are sexually diverse or gender-diverse. One of my wife's LDS colleagues knocked on our door late one Thursday night after her twenty-year-old brother came out to her as gay. After several hours of talking and processing, she said, "I think Heavenly Father placed the two of you in my life to prepare me for this moment," and then she spent the next several years carefully shepherding her entire extended Latine/Latinx family to an unequivocal acceptance of her brother (and now his life partner).

And at the same time, I have taught hundreds of current and former LDS students who have been deeply wounded by the church's teachings on sexuality and gender, and by their own family members. I have witnessed students being expelled by their families after coming out as sexually diverse or gender-diverse. I have listened to students describe the trauma of "conversion therapies" aimed at eliminating same-gender attractions. I have listened to students describe how their marriages failed nearly immediately after they began, when one partner discovered that marriage could not "cure" their "pathology." The essays in this volume speak to this broad spectrum of experiences—pain, relief, support, abandonment, confusion, clarity. Each individual has had to navigate their own path toward self-love, companionship, and spirituality. Sometimes alone, sometimes with help. Sometimes within the church, sometimes not. Sometimes in intersection with other forms of marginalization. These are not finished journeys—they are portraits of lives *in the process of being lived*, and it is a privilege and an honor to witness the power and vulnerability of each and every story.

Lisa Diamond
Professor of Psychology and Gender Studies
University of Utah

INTRODUCTION

Kerry Spencer Pray and Jenn Lee Smith

A couple years ago, I (Kerry) went to a dinner for LGBTQ Mormons. My wife and I sat at a table with a pathologist and with the founder of a biotech company. We talked about AIDS, about how the treatments were developed, why it took so long, how they work. As we talked, two gay men in their 60s came and sat at the table with us and I realized: the only gay men over sixty I personally knew were from spaces like this—gay Mormons who had stayed largely closeted during the AIDS crisis. Men who were celibate.

I don't believe in celibacy, particularly not as a mass prescription for any group of people. Humans are mammals who are not, as a general rule, meant to be alone. Celibacy hurts most of us. Being in the closet hurts us. And so it was difficult to hold these two facts at once: something that had denied these men their humanity had saved them. But it was society's denial of their humanity that put them in danger. We could have treated AIDS *years* sooner. But the sick men weren't seen as being worthy of saving because they were gay. Rooms and rooms, queer space upon queer space, empty of an entire generation because we did not value their humanity.

At some point, my wife turned to me. "We're the only gay women in this room right now," she said. "Get on your phone, get some others here!"

I just looked at her. "I . . . can't," I said.

"Sure you can."

"No, you don't understand. There isn't anyone for me to call."

"Where are the other gay Mormon women?" she asked. "Don't tell me there aren't any."

I stared at her in horror. There are gay Mormon women, but most stay closeted. Most stay in their mixed-orientation marriages. They don't come to events for support. I thought of a secret Facebook group I'm in. Of the women, desperate, suicidal, who won't leave their marriages because they don't want to hurt or embarrass their husbands. Female anguish in Mormon culture means nothing next to male discomfort. The "important" queer Mormon voices? They are almost always male, cisgender, and gay. And so I found myself in a room, empty of women, because our humanity wasn't seen as important. My wife got really upset. We had to make an excuse to leave.

This sort of absence, the erasure of an entire group of people, is a common experience in the queer Mormon community. Like many other belief systems, Mormonism is hierarchical, essentialist, and patriarchal. It is bad at dealing with people who don't fit its prescriptive norms.

The experience of being a queer Mormon is both similar and dissimilar to the experience of other queer people of faith. While Mormonism can be historically situated within the sects of Christianity that arose from what scholars call the "Second Great Awakening," which was, as historian Paul E. Johnson says, a time of "hundreds of strange religious events that occurred all across the United States from the 1820s to the 1840s,"[1] it has grown into a unique cultural and political force within modern America. Many splinter groups arose from Joseph Smith's original church and can accurately be called Mormon, but this book generally refers to the largest, which is known as the Church of Jesus Christ of Latter-day Saints. As of 2019, this sect reported a worldwide membership in excess of 16.5 million. Additionally, it boasts disproportionately large representation in the politics of the United States. In 2021, there were nine Mormon congressmen, including three senators.

Much of the rhetoric against queer people in the Mormon Church is based in a document called "The Family: A Proclamation to the World." Written in 1995, the Proclamation was specifically created to be used in a legal setting, establishing heteronormativity as central to Mormonism. It was intended to be used to combat the normalization of same-sex relationships and argue against same-sex marriage on moral grounds. Scholar Taylor Petrey notes that one of the most important things about the Proclamation is that it is not a particularly Mormon document. It was written with a political agenda and is similar to documents of other faiths from the Christian religious right. "The Proclamation," he says, "shared a number of features with these other documents, like verbal formulas, topics, and structure." One example of this was "in 1988 [when] Jerry Falwell's Moral Majority, Phyllis Schlafly's Eagle Forum, James Dobson's Family Research Council, and other institutions of the Religious Right jointly released a policy document titled 'Family Manifesto.'"[2]

To eschew variations on gender and orientation in favor of a hetero-nuclear model is, thus, not a uniquely Mormon approach. However, Mormonism varies in its approach to queerness in distinct ways. While other Christian groups have produced documents similar to the Proclamation and employed scripture-based rhetoric to encourage strict gender roles, Mormonism elevates the hetero-nuclear family to the level of a saving ordinance. Marriage has long been central to the Mormon faith. In 1843, in the Mormon scriptures known as the Doctrine and Covenants, marriage is called a "new and everlasting covenant" and those who are unwilling to accept the covenant are condemned: "for no one can reject this covenant and be permitted to enter into [God's] glory."[3] While this scripture specifically was referring to the practice of *plural* marriage, when the church disavowed the practice of plural marriage in 1890, ritual sealings (Mormon temple marriage ceremonies) continued to refer to marriage as the "new and everlasting covenant" and marriage continued to be considered fundamentally requisite for salvation.

This salvific approach to (implicitly and explicitly heteronormative) marriage makes the acceptance of queer Mormons fundamentally untenable on a doctrinal level. Furthermore, Mormonism as practiced by The Church of Jesus Christ of Latter-day Saints is much more centralized and authority-based than other Christian religions. While non-Mormons may be allowed to find a more accepting parish, Mormons are assigned into a parish, or *ward*, by geography and deviations are not permitted. Groups of wards are geographically situated into *stakes*. A ward is led by a bishop and a stake is led by a president, both of whom interact with and act as judges for members. This leads to a phenomenon colloquially known as "leadership roulette." While some queer Mormons may be lucky to have a bishop who is accepting of queer identities, those who are in wards with unaccepting leadership do not have the ability to leave. As much of the practice of Mormonism relies on direct interaction with leadership—temple attendance, for example, requires that you prove yourself "worthy" and the issuance of the "temple recommends" required for entrance into the sacred spaces is predicated upon passing a series of interviews with both your bishop and stake president—this inflexibility often leaves queer Mormons in conflict with leadership. The cost of rejection from the temple is particularly high: the Mormon concept of sealing asserts an errant child could be separated eternally from the rest of the family. On a doctrinal level, queerness represents an existential threat not only to the salvation of the individual, but to the celestial family.

Female queerness is in particular anathema to Mormonism. The central leadership of the Mormon Church is organized around the concept of priesthood authority. The authority by which a bearer may perform ecclesiastical acts of service in the name of God is called priesthood. It is available to boys starting at the age of 12. Women are never ordained to the priesthood in Mormonism and gain access to it only through their husbands, other male church members, and, in limited ways, in temple worship. While some women do hold positions of some authority in the Mormon Church, they are always subject to the priesthood authority, which is always male. The Relief Society, which is the women's organization in the church, is nominally led by women, but those women are subject to male authority. The president of the church, the apostles, and other general authorities are all male. Women are dependent upon their relationships with men—specifically marriage to men—for salvation.

This strict division between men and women in the Mormon faith, one reinforced by the institution's organization and power structure, causes problems for queer people in the church who do not easily fit and leads to blindspots when it comes to the representation of queer people. One such blindspot that profoundly affects queer people in the Mormon Church is the inability to see anything other than binary gender.

When we first started to seek out the experiences of other queer Mormon women, we were surprised at the degree to which our own entrenchment in Mormon culture limited the way we searched. We still thought in binaries—after all, that is what Mormonism taught us to do. We looked for other *women*. But the reality is, our ontologies are far more complex than the simple, essentialist binaries preached in a Mormon chapel. The voices of cis men are privileged in Mormonism and the voices of women are marginalized—this is beyond argument. But the strict binaries result in the complete *erasure* of so many other people. We had been taught to think of two distinct groups—men and women—when the lived reality of gender is far more complex, and the scope of erasure far more all-encompassing. We are all affected by the implicit misogyny in Mormon spaces, but not all of the victims are women.

This is illustrated not only by the lack of women in common queer Mormon spaces, but also in the lack of trans men in those same spaces. I (Kerry) was recently talking to my friend, Kimberly Anderson, who is a trans woman. We'd just been on a Zoom call, filled mainly with trans Mormon women. I was talking about how I didn't apply to anywhere except Brigham Young University (BYU), partly because that's where my parents thought I should go. "My mom said I wasn't allowed to work, because women aren't supposed to work," I told her. "And I wasn't allowed to go into debt, so I had to get scholarships."

"Wait," she said. "Wait, go back. Women work. Women do *so much* work, but just sit with that for a second. Just acknowledge the implicit implication nothing women could do could ever be considered *work*."

"Women aren't allowed to acknowledge a lot of things about themselves," I said.

"I think a lot about how there are so many more trans women than trans men who come to things like that Zoom call," she said. "And I think it's partly because we were *raised* as male, even if we weren't. No one ever told us we should make ourselves smaller, that we weren't as important."

The intersection of culture and gender is so particularly fraught within Mormonism not only because of this intense gender binary, but because of the way the enforcement of the gender binary was linked to white supremacy. Since the postwar era when the church began to actively seek to limit both racial integration and gender-role expansion, the gender binary was seen as a way to preserve and protect the family. Petrey explains, "Like racial difference, [the church] regarded sexual difference as divinely ordained. Like racial difference, sexual difference was also at risk of dissolution amid the cultural changes of the era. Like racial difference, church leaders believed sexual difference was hierarchical. And like racial difference, church leaders believed that sexual difference was necessary to protect the proper transmission and exercise of the priesthood."[4] The power structures of the church in this era evolved in a way that even more strictly centralized power among white men. Petrey notes, "Male church leaders instituted several programs to ensure that the proper household patriarchal order would be carried out—and that gender roles would be maintained."[5]

Harold B. Lee led something called, "The Priesthood Correlation Committee" and throughout the 1960s, "Correlation leadership slowly weakened the Relief Society, stripping it of its budget, its independent publications, and its active Social Services agency. A goal of this movement was to diminish women's authority in the church in deference to the male priesthood."[6] The priesthood was not extended to include Black men until 1978 and, thus, Correlation entrenched restrictions on both gender and race. Females and Blacks could speak only with permission from the men above them, and they lost that permission the moment their words threatened the white patriarchal power structure. And while Black men have since been included into the Priesthood authority, there have never been any Black prophets or apostles, just as there have never been any female, nonbinary, or openly queer Mormon prophets or apostles. There is no room in Mormonism for anything other than *male* and *female*, and the people with power are largely cis, male, and white. It is hard for marginalized queer Mormons not to internalize this.

Lisa Diamond, psychologist and feminist author of *Sexual Fluidity: Understanding Women's Love and Desire* writes that "Girls internalize cultural and social factors, which then shape their experiences of sexuality at a deep level."[7] As screenwriter and activist, Dustin Lance Black notes in his essay, "Mustangs and Mama Dragons," Mormon culture is particularly repressive for those it calls women: "The truth of the Church then and still today is that women exist to serve their husbands and are discouraged from any ambition besides having and raising children."[8] Greg Prince points out in *Gay Rights and The Mormon Church*, "the general focus of church leaders on male homosexuality . . . is consistent with a misogyny that is apparent both on a broad scale . . . and on a narrow one" given the gendered nature of leadership roles and general invisibility of women in the Church of Jesus Christ of Latter-day Saints.[9] People of color, trans, queer, lesbian, and nonbinary Mormons gather in the sidelines of meetings and conferences, hearing from and about cisgender, gay, often white men.

A search of EBSCO academic databases for "Queer Mormon" includes research about the religious experiences of gay men—for example the work of Bradshaw and colleagues—but no similar examination of the experiences of women, of trans Mormons, or of nonbinary Mormons.[10] In spite of what the databases would indicate, these experiences are more common than is acknowledged. In a widespread study of contemporary Mormonism, researchers included an "other" option for gender and were so surprised at the number of responses they got, they separated the results into a second study, exploring the way the religion contributes to the "cisgendering" of worldview.[11] In spite of the fact that "queer" is a label that resists specification of gender or orientation—scholar J. Walker even makes a compelling argument, using Judith Butler's definitions of queerness, that nineteenth-century Mormons, as a whole people, can be reasonably labeled queer[12]— queer Mormon research does not tend to include investigation outside of binary gender. The Lefevor study, which notes, "the majority of participants were young (60.9% under 40), men (69.6%), White (93.0%), and well-educated (66.1% having a bachelor's degree or higher)" is not alone in the world of queer Mormon research.[13] Survey-based research relies on the ability and willingness of people to self-identify or to participate in queer spaces. The Lovell study on queer Mormons, which used prominent Facebook groups known to "cater to LGBTQ/SSA Mormons" was only able to recruit 16 women, compared to 40 men, largely because women do not frequent public queer Mormon spaces to the same degree men do.[14]

Even the assumptions made by those studying Mormonism reflect the privileging of cis gay male voices. In a review of Prince's book, *Gay Rights and the Mormon Church*, Jaclyn Foster notes that while Prince acknowledges the dearth of non-cis-gay-male voices within Mormonism, he still demonstrates the same implicit eschewing of those voices: "Prince focuses on gay men even when his source base does not constrain him," she says. This is illustrated in the fact that his "review of the scientific literature, 'The Biology of Homosexuality,' only cites studies on gay men."[15]

Patriarchy, strict gender binaries, repression of female sexual desire in the doctrine, and outright misogyny are only a few of the barriers that keep those of marginalized genders and orientations silent. The language of gender in Mormonism is so strong and so binary we don't always have the ability to recognize more than "the priesthood" and "everyone else." There is male and there is female, there are people in power and people not in power. Women and children in one room, men in the other.

This means many queer Mormons do not even have the language with which to name their queerness until it becomes critical. And this can often happen when they are already in marriages, have already been raising children, when they have—as they have been instructed—chosen to eschew careers and focus on parenthood. They simply do not have the ability to act on their queerness. Secret Facebook groups are filled with queer Mormons who are closeted with no hope of ever coming out of the closet. Their anguish is not enough to give them the ability.

There is a growing body of work around the mental health of LGBTQ Mormons with some focusing on people other than cisgender males. In a 2014 survey of cisgender women who identified as Mormon experiencing same-sex sexuality, Jeanna Jacobsen found that "participants reported deep struggles and feelings of isolation, worthlessness, and loss due to conflicting identities shaped by religious beliefs and sexuality."[16] The most significant loss that women in this study experienced was the loss of religious community and the role of community in their lives. Jacobsen suggests in another study that beyond healing through healthy self-concept and critical support from therapists, family, and friends, "advocacy is needed for safer spaces within religious communities."[17] Allies play an important role in building safe spaces within existing communities, and in helping to build new spaces outside of existing communities.

Shifting into different communities can provoke deep questions about identity and place within Mormonism. These questions are harder to answer without the right language. Lovell discusses the way we learn to define our identities within a Mormon and wider context: "sexuality, social movements, religious creeds, and other social meanings are in dialogue with each other as an individual makes sense of their sexual attractions and experiences."[18] But when a culture lacks the language to discuss something—through taboo, shame or even just an unwillingness to entertain a dialogue outside the narrative of heteronormativity—the language becomes stilted and people are less able to situate themselves within both their culture and their sexuality or gender identity. Petrey notes that within the church, queerness has been thought of as homosexuality, and homosexuality has been "conceived of as a problem for men."[19] Scholar and writer Alan Michael Williams says, "the issue of homosexuality for the Church, is, at its core, about gender," and it threatens the nature of priesthood ordination.[20] This is true for all sorts of queerness within Mormonism.

The result is the life stories of many queer Mormons have largely been rendered invisible. Trans, intersex, agender, and nonbinary people are obscured by the church's insistence on essential binary genders. Cis women who are attracted to women are subject to myriad denials of women's sexuality. As a result, they commonly marry men and have children before fully realizing their queerness. All of us who are marginalized in the church's patriarchy have reason to leave. Ongoing racism, sexism, transphobia, and homophobia from both institution and community compound with harmful beliefs we learn and internalize about ourselves. And yet the reasons to stay can feel equally compelling: our families, communities, identities as Mormons, and testimonies don't go away because the church does not have a place for us.

There are so many things Mormons of marginalized genders and orientations could say, but we don't always have the following:

- The words. The language and awareness to name it.
- The ability. By the time queerness is self-known, many people are in marriages with children. They may have sacrificed their own careers for the careers of their spouses. There is a great deal to lose in coming out and the gains may not be readily apparent.
- The context. Cultural constructions of gender exist in opposition to biological realities of gender, particularly within the Mormon Church.
- The power. The priesthood has the power. The "other" does not. These voices are systematically silenced.
- The safety. Often, this is literal.

At a certain point, the whys become less expedient in the face of a total *absence* of a voice. What we need are the voices. What we need are the stories. Even if they are halting, even if they are unskilled, even if they will never be free from the cultural strings that shape their choices and assumptions, we need to know they are there.

This book is a collection of essays written by people of marginalized genders—trans men and women, cis women, nonbinary and agender people—marginalized sexual orientations—bisexual, lesbian, asexual, queer, pansexual—and people with intersex characteristics. The collection also addresses the experience of queer Mormons as it intersects with race, ethnicity, and nationality. The persistent stigma faced by people of marginalized genders manifests, at times, in the things our authors are and are not willing to say. While our list of authors includes some who are intersex, for example, intersex traits, in particular, were something they did not address in this volume. We hope that the existence of this book lessens stigma enough that future volumes are able to more fully address this aspect of sex and how it intersects with gender.

The stories we've included are mostly not from professional writers. They're from ordinary queer and trans people; a community of people who have not always had the words or training to talk about their experiences. This changes the way readers will want to interpret and interact with the prose. Many of our writers are writing anonymously from the closet. The ability of our authors to write with anonymity was important to us. Without their ability to stay in the closet, you might not hear so many of these stories. And we wanted to share the stories that aren't told. From voices you don't hear.

We chose the narrative form because we aren't looking at the why, we're just looking at the what. This is our life, these are our lives, this is how we have spent our time. The narrative form relies less on introspection and more on action. I am here, in this place, this is what I'm doing and this is how I am spending my hours.

We divided the essays into four parts:

- essays on identity
- essays on relationships
- essays on shame/suicide/the closet
- essays on the church

Each section will be preceded by a short introduction, giving some context for the essays.

One thing these essays have in common is the subsuming sense of *silence*. Queer Mormons of marginalized genders and orientations are trying to navigate who they are in a church that does not talk about them, within structures that don't value their voices, without the right words to describe their experiences. The very Mormonism of our authors leaves them at a loss for articulating the reality of their lived experience at times. As we worked with authors to edit their essays, we were sometimes left with a strange paradox: we had to encourage authors to edit things out of their essays that actually illustrated the very Mormoness of them. "You never acknowledge your own queerness," we said to one author. "You talk about other people's queerness, but never your own." To another author, we said, "You don't actually object to this treatment anywhere. You keep trying to make this OK. *Don't try to make this OK.*" There's a sense that speaking is what breaks things in Mormonism. Contention is, at all costs, to be avoided. But some things need to be broken.

Audre Lorde ends her essay titled "The Transformation of Silence into Language and Action" by stating, "The fact that we are here and that I speak these words is an attempt to break that silence and bridge some of those differences between us, for it is not difference which immobilizes us, but silence. And there are so many silences to be broken."[21]

This anthology is just the beginning of breaking that silence. Within this silence is a sea of other silences. If you are a reader wondering, why is my voice not represented here? Let us know. For several years we have been collecting stories through our blog, qmwproject.com, and we would love to hear your stories, as well.

Joanna Brooks wrote, "Our stories are not told in sacred books. They are not told over the pulpit. They are not told by the prophets. No one says: I felt my church turn away from me, and it was a kind of death. . . . No one says any of these things. But they should. Because no one should be left to believe that she is the only one. No one should be left to believe that she is the only Mormon girl who walked alone into the dark."[22]

Queer Mormon women, trans Mormons, asexual Mormons, nonbinary, agender, and gender diverse Mormons should not have to believe they are alone.

We are, none of us, alone.

NOTES

1. Paul E. Johnson and Sean Wilentz, *The Kingdom of Matthias: A Story of Sex and Salvation in 19th-Century America* (New York: Oxford University Press, 2012), 6.
2. Taylor G. Petrey, *Tabernacles of Clay: Sexuality and Gender in Modern Mormonism* (Chapel Hill: The University of North Carolina Press, 2020), 145.
3. D&C 132:4.
4. Petrey, *Tabernacles of Clay*, 32.
5. Petrey, *Tabernacles of Clay*, 37.
6. Petrey, *Tabernacles of Clay*, 37.
7. Lisa M. Diamond, *Sexual Fluidity: Understanding Women's Love and Desire* (Cambridge, MA: Harvard University Press, 2008), 21.
8. Dustin Lance Black, "Mustangs and Mama Dragons," in *The Book of Queer Prophets*, ed. Ruth Hunt (London: William Collins, 2020), 68.
9. Gregory Prince, *Gay Rights and the Mormon Church* (Salt Lake City: University of Utah Press, 2019), 120.
10. W.S. Bradshaw, T.B. Heaton, E. Decoo, J.P. Dehlin, R.V. Galliher, and K.A. Crowell, "Religious Experiences of GBTQ Mormon Males," *Journal for the Scientific Study of Religion* 54, no. 2 (2015): 311–29.
11. J.E. Sumerau, Ryan T. Cragun, and Lain A.B. Mathers, "Contemporary Religion and the Cisgendering of Reality," *Social Currents* 3, no. 3 (2016): 293–311.

12. J. Walker, "Queer Mormonism: Deuterocanonicity and Discursive Subversion," *English Language Notes* 50, no. 2 (2012): 129.

13. G. T. Lefevor, I.P. Blaber, C.E. Huffman, et al., "The Role of Religiousness and Beliefs about Sexuality in Well-Being Among Sexual Minority Mormons," *Psychology of Religion and Spirituality* (June 2019): 12.

14. E. Lovell, "Queering Mormonism and Mormonizing Sexuality: The Intersectionality and Hybridity of Conflicting Identities," *Conference Papers—American Sociological Association* (January 2016): 16.

15. Jaclyn Foster, "Gay Rights and the Mormon Church: Intended Actions, Unintended Consequences" (Review), *Utah Historical Quarterly* 88, no. 3 (Summer 2020): 256.

16. Jeanna Jacobsen and Rachel Wright, "Mental Health Implications in Mormon Women's Experiences with Same-Sex Attraction: A Qualitative Study," *The Counselling Psychologist* 42, no. 5 (2014): 689.

17. Jeanna Jacobsen, "Community Influences on Mormon Women with Same-Sex Sexuality." *Culture, Health, and Sexuality* 19, no. 12 (2017): 1325.

18. E. Lovell, "Queering Mormonism," 3.

19. Petrey, *Tabernacles of Clay*, 102.

20. Alan Michael Williams, "Mormon and Queer at the Crossroads," *Dialogue: A Journal of Mormon Thought* 44, no. 1 (2011): 67.

21. Audre Lorde, "The Transformation of Silence into Language and Action," in *Sister Outsider* (New York: Crossing Press, 2007), 44.

22. Joanna Brooks, *The Book of Mormon Girl: A Memoir of an American Faith* (New York: Free Press, 2012), 143–44.

Essays on Identity

Introduction to Part I

Jenn Lee Smith

> Part of our spiritual independence is simply shaking off wrongful
> messages about who we are. We get them from people who don't
> know us but who judge us, from people who restrict us from being
> who we are.
>
> —Chieko Okazaki, first person of color to serve in the
> presidency of an LDS Church auxiliary organization.[1]

Many queer Mormons hesitate to come out for fear of further marginalization. If they are not able-bodied, not white, not cisgender, not male, they
might fear having to add "not straight" on top of an already full plate of
powerlessness and invisibility. The voices in "Essays on Identity" point to a
profound strength found in deep reflection and, often, prayer at the place
where one's identity—which longs to be whole—is cracked and splintered.
A certain vigilance and faith are required to pull these pieces of the self
together and then to persistently state one's truth in hopes that it might
be heard and honored.

Queer Mormon spaces, to their credit, strive to be all-inclusive. Often,
however, they still perpetuate belief systems grounded in the sticky systems
of white supremacy and patriarchy. Because these systems are so embedded,
I believe the people within these spaces do not intend to be so isolating. Most
do not fully comprehend why their organizations are not safe enough for
those on the outside. Queer Mormons and Mormon-adjacent people who are
trans, ace, nonbinary, disabled, and people of color find one another and ask,
"Without our shared queer/religious oppression, would they even notice or
think about us?" Learning to live in a more visible way does not come easily,
and yet, many are leading by example and creating their own spaces.

There is no easy way to escape the discomfort and trauma of conflicting identities. The stories in this section speak to the mental, physical, emotional, and spiritual exhaustion of individuals holding on to sacred truths. Several authors speak to being Mormon as the largest part of their identity. They detail winding journeys plagued with self-doubt and compartmentalizing pieces of one's identity in order to survive. According to present church doctrine, certain identities are eternal, which presents a challenge for those of us who fall between essentializing categories.

In describing the precarious balance of identities, queer Mormons often cite the traumatizing effect of "The Policy of Exclusion," or POX as it is colloquially known. On November 5, 2015, the church quietly updated the rules in its leadership handbook, declaring that people in same-sex partnerships were apostates and/or subject to excommunication; that their children would be excluded from baptism prior to age eighteen.[2] In the wake of the POX, we struggled to navigate our identities knowing that our children would be rejected for our queerness. When the policy was reversed in 2019, with similarly little fanfare, we were left with unreconciled feelings of rejection and no better sense of where we fit into the larger community of the church.[3]

For those with multiple marginalities, there is an added level of complexity. Valerie Purdie-Vaughns and Richard P. Eibach argue that the experience of having a marginalized identity within an androcentric group like Mormonism is one that, inevitably, leads to erasure. Those who have intersecting identities "tend to be marginal members within marginalized groups. This status relegates them to a position of acute social invisibility."[4] Silent and invisible may be what is expected of sexual and gender minorities in this religion, but agency remains an important doctrine in Mormonism. The ability and privilege God gives all people to choose and act as their authentic selves is exercised by the contributors of this book in not just their willingness to share vulnerable truths, but also in chosen names that better reflect their identities.

In my search for ways to better understand intersecting and fluid identities, I am inspired by the lived experiences of feminist scholars such as Kathy Rudy, who shares personal anecdotes of a time in the 1980s when feminist communities were forced to acknowledge that what they were building excluded women of color. While a predominantly queer community was more open to racial differences, the overall feminist methods of study and discourse around intersections of marginalities were insufficient to make room for everyone's lived experiences. "The real problem," Rudy said, "has been how feminist theory has confused the condition of one group of women with the condition of all."[5]

The book that most shaped my queer feminist identity is *This Bridge Called My Back*, an anthology of essays, letters, and poetry by Native

American, Latinx, Black, and Asian American folx many of whom identify as lesbian. Published in 1981, it was edited by Cherríe Moraga and Gloria Anzaldua. After being in too many rooms with too few people doing the work of translating, bridging, and mediating, Chicana lesbian and feminist activist Moraga describes the felt experience of marginality within a feminism that excludes women of color: "the exhaustion we feel in our bones at the end of the day, the fire we feel in our hearts when we are insulted, the knife we feel in our backs when we are betrayed." She adds, "At home, amongst ourselves, women of color ask the political question: *what about us?* Which really means: *what about* all *of us?*"[6]

To recognize the intrinsic and paradoxical complexities in each of our stories is to move towards the wholeness and completeness and truth of all our stories. It is to shed the layers of what we've been told we ought to be. Scholar and activist bell hooks was taught by the elders in her community that, "to be fully self-actualized [is] the only way to truly heal."[7] Healing comes as we shake off wrongful messages about who we are and instead, share our stories in places of safety among listeners who believe us. Healing comes when we break our own silences and, in turn, honor the voices that we would otherwise not hear and value. In this chapter, we hear from a mother raising her children to be free of shame, women born in male bodies, folx finding congruence in new names and new haircuts. These stories of identities are not stagnant. They are ever evolving and fluid. Here in each story is a slice of one's journey through identities that move toward greater healing and self-actualization.

NOTES

1. Chieko Okazaki, *Lighten Up! Finding Real Joy in Life* (Salt Lake City: Deseret Book, 1993), 100.
2. Laurie Goodstein, "New Policy on Gay Couples and their Children Roils Mormon Church," *New York Times,* Nov. 13, 2015, https://www.nytimes.com/2015/11/14/us/mormons-set-to-quit-church-over-policy-on-gay-couples-and-their-children.html.
3. Sarah Pulliam Bailey, "Mormon Church to Allow Baptisms, Blessings for Children of LGBT Parents, Reversing 2015 Policy," *Washington Post,* April 4, 2019, https://www.washingtonpost.com/religion/2019/04/04/mormon-church-allow-baptisms-blessings-children-lgbt-parents-reversing-policy/.
4. Valerie Purdie-Vaughns and Richard P. Eibach, "Intersectional Invisibility: The Distinctive Advantages and Disadvantages of Multiple Subordinate-Group Identities," *Sex Roles* 59, no. 5–6 (2008): 381.
5. Kathy Rudy. "Radical Feminism, Lesbian Separatism, and Queer Theory," *Feminist Studies* 27, no. 1 (April 1, 2001): 191–222.
6. Cherríe Moraga and Gloria Anzaldua, eds., *This Bridge Called My Back: Writings by Radical Women of Color* (Albany, NY: SUNY Press, 2015): xix.
7. bell hooks, *Belonging: A Culture of Place* (New York: Routledge, 2009): 21.

The Thing about Secrets

Amanda Farr

I can remember lurking in the corner of the BYU library, way back in the winter of 2004, reading some of the very first posts on Feminist Mormon Housewives. Those posts threw me into a new world and way of thinking, and as a result, I have these angsty, deeply emotional, ridiculously earnest journal entries from that time. One in particular sticks out in my mind, and I can best sum it up by sharing that I ended that entry with the sincere, yet possibly dramatic, question, "Maybe God answers prayers with feminists?" That was me.

I'm so Mormon, my high school nickname was "Mormon." I'm so Mormon, I stayed in on Friday nights so I could make flashcards for the Stake Seminary Scripture Chase. I mean, flashcards are nerdy in and of themselves, but scripture flashcards? Even I knew I was pushing it. (As an aside and for the record, I kicked trash at those scripture chases.) I'm so Mormon, I planned what I was wearing to the next stake dance on the way home from the stake dance. Am I making my point? Don't worry, I can keep going. I'm so Mormon, I went to Girls Camp with two different stakes on more than one occasion. And not like, bi-stake girls camp. No. Like a week with one stake, and an additional week with another stake. Every single summer. Although, now that I'm thinking about it, that might have had more to do with the whole being gay thing. I don't want to rewrite history or anything, but it's entirely possible I may not have understood my motivations to attend.

I'm so Mormon, I went to the Hill Cumorah[1] for my high school senior week trip. I did this voluntarily, and I did it with genuine excitement. I loved sitting in sacred spaces, honoring the space that has shaped and influenced and touched so many before me. I'm so Mormon, I didn't need to google how to spell Cumorah while writing this out. The point is, for a young girl growing up in western Pennsylvania, where my stake was easily a three-hour drive from boundary to boundary, being Mormon was the largest part of my identity. I wasn't just a Mormon. I was Mormon.

So it will come as no surprise that I did what many young Mormon women do—I set my sights on the temple. That sacred, not secret, place we all strove to enter someday. The temple, I was told, could "fix" the things that were testing my faith. Like, maybe perhaps, my ever-present attraction to women. I don't even think I could name it as an attraction, the way I could name the articles of faith, or list the prophets, or sing "Come, Come, Ye Saints" but I knew it was there. I knew it was testing me. I knew I couldn't say it out loud. It was my secret.

It wasn't sacred. I knew that sacred means the temple and I knew that the temple is holy. The temple isn't a sinister secret. The reason we don't talk about the temple is because it is sanctified, divine, the House of the Lord. But my secret? There were other, much more pernicious reasons for not talking about that. And so I buried my secret deep within myself. I carried it with me everywhere, because that's the thing about secrets. We have to hold them. People don't place secrets on a shelf, people keep secrets. They aren't given away. Secrets are to be tightly held, kept under wraps. The temple, the sacred, that is what we are to seek out, to search for, to find and honor in our life. In my supremely Mormon brain, very simply put, if the sacred was good, then I knew the secret must be bad. I broke it down into something black and white, a Truth with a capital "T."

The fullness of the gospel. And the gospel that I loved so much—it was the Good Word. The Word that taught us to mourn with those who mourn and comfort those who stand in need of comfort. What a gracious and holy teaching. Even now, my bones warm with the phrase. The Good Word, which taught us the greatest way for us to be like Him, that radical-Jewish-teacher-become-Savior, was to consecrate ourselves and to devote ourselves to those around us. The Word was good. And the Word was who I was. But that secret. That secret was also who I was. And I knew it was bad; I knew it definitely was not sacred.

There was nothing sacred about my secret. Who I was, who I loved; I couldn't help but process all of that as bad. As unclean. Unwanted. Unworthy. All of these parts of me: the Mormon part of me and the secret part of me, they all sought peace inside a tumultuous place. There was none to be found. For a long time, I thought the tighter I clung to my secret, the smaller it would become. It was a paper ball that I crumpled up in my fist, squeezing it tighter and tighter. It was now dirty from my palms and grossly covered in sweat. But try as I might—temple marriage, Relief Society presidency, babies and adoption and filling out food orders and service projects and all things sacred—I couldn't manage to crumple that secret into a ball small enough to disappear. It's funny, what happens when you carry something around for so long. In the beginning, you think you can do it forever. "It's just a ball of paper," I would whisper to myself. Tiny, barely perceptible. But year after year, it seemed to grow instead of shrink. My arms began to ache and my heart struggled to function under the growing burden. And one day, my body broke, and my secret came tumbling out.

I was gay. There it was. This secret I refused to name, this burden I tried so hard to carry. Suddenly it was there, no longer hidden in my clenched fist, just there. Out in the world: dirty and covered in my vulnerabilities. Lying open for everyone to see and judge. Broken, I stood up and prepared to count and measure myself. I was prepared to definitively see myself as broken. I faced my own image and I saw someone good. Someone who loved the people around her. Someone who served her community. Someone who mourned and comforted not only because she had been taught to do so, but because that was the person she was. Someone who fought for a safer world for the children in her home. And it didn't make sense—because this part of me was supposed to be bad, but . . . it wasn't.

For the first time, I realized the only thing bad about my secret was that I was keeping it. It took so much practice to stop keeping that secret. First, only to myself in the mirror, and then tiny parts of it to trusted, beloved friends and many, many tear-filled conversations with my now ex-husband. There were some terrible conversations with family and overwhelmingly loving conversations with friends. And finally, the whole truth to the whole world. I am a gay Mormon woman. I am Mormon. And I am gay. And all of those identities are sacred. All are holy. All are anointed truths that make me who I am.

As a mother, I look at my children, and I see the freedom with which they live. They have somehow escaped these scary secrets about their identities. My daughter, Charlotte, now seven years old, had no fear when I came out to her. She quickly and unabashedly questioned me, "Uhhh, do I have to be gay? I don't want to be gay." As I assured her that she could absolutely be straight, she shrugged her shoulders and said, "Well, okay then," and promptly left to go play with Barbies. She knows I don't love Barbies. She knows that she does. She knows who she is. Nothing about Charlotte is a secret.

My nine-year-old lives in a world where being genderqueer is accepted and quite frankly, expected. A world where when the game console asks a group of fourth grade boys to "select a gender" and only offers male/female, they independently, and rather academically, discuss the follies of a gender binary and the ridiculousness of needing to declare their gender on an Xbox profile. "As if it even matters," they scoff.

I know, my babies are young, and they will come with a new generation of secrets. But I pray the lesson they will learn from me is that the energy we use to hold those secrets so tight, ultimately becomes the power those secrets have over our lives. Who we are and who we love: those truths are sacred. I can preach all day about letting go of secrets. The truth is, I still keep them. I keep them for me—little ones, like where I hide the Oreos, and larger ones about mistakes I have made and people I have hurt along my journey.

But I still find myself keeping certain truths secret in some effort to protect that other sacred identity that I have: Mormon. I drive by my former ward building, and from the back seat, my four-year-old pipes up, "That's our church! Why don't we go anymore?" and the seven-year-old asks, "Yeah, Mom, why did they kick you out?" And I sit in silence. I still don't have the heart to share that secret. It stays tightly held, a weight in my hand and a lump in my throat. I still haven't found the courage to open my fist, and let that secret fall out. I cannot turn around and look them in their perfect eyes and say, "It wasn't just me they rejected. It was you."

NOTE

1. The Hill Cumorah is the site where Joseph Smith, the founder of the Mormon faith, said he discovered the golden plates, which he translated into the Book of Mormon. The Book of Mormon is the primary volume of Mormon scripture. Other scriptural texts include the Joseph Smith translation of the Bible, the Doctrine and Covenants, and the Pearl of Great Price. From 1935 to 2019, the Hill Cumorah was the site of a large "pageant": a theatrical performance featuring stories from the Book of Mormon.

Memoir of a *Wikta*
Naji Haska Runs Through

2

I was born on December 17, 2001, in Cedar City, Utah, as a new member to the Assiniboine tribe. My federal name is Naji Haska Runs Through. When I was born, my family was going through a hard time. Mother says the sound of my laugh and my first smile out of the womb made any following trials worth it. I am the fifth son and the last of her seven children to come into the world. While my parents were still together at the time, she had a sinking feeling that she would be raising me on her own. As a child, I would wear tutus and play with dolls. My favorite was the traditional Assiniboine doll my mother made. It was hand sewn, stuffed with buffalo hair, decorated with glass beads, with a body of hide and a head of hair from a horse's mane.

I called her Blue Bird Woman, after a character from my favorite movie to watch as a child, Hallmark's *Dreamkeeper*. It's a five-hour miniseries that I watched on repeat like other toddlers watched the latest Disney blockbuster. *Dreamkeeper* is about a boy and his grandfather on their way to the Gathering of Nations powwow in Albuquerque, New Mexico. On their journey, his grandfather tells traditional stories of the First Nation people in North America. I related to the Native women and their traditional roles in the old societies. Often it felt as though I was projecting myself on the doll my mother made me.

As I grew older, I became more aware of the spirits trapped inside my body. My mother always told me that she would love me no matter what I became and would be there for whatever I needed. She raised me in the Church of Jesus Christ of Latter-day Saints, where I first found comfort in God. Despite the homophobia and transphobia exhibited by the saints around me, I knew they were not evil but misguided, as humans often are. Instead of allowing the few bigots to affect me, I tried to focus on the support from those in my ward who have watched me grow up. They see me for the beautiful and creative person I've become, and genuinely love me for who I am.

Dealing with the traditional genders of my people and those of my religion has always been complex. The feelings of acceptance from a community vanishing and the feeling of ignorance from a community that is growing every day has caused turmoil in my earthly body. I feel pressure from others to categorize myself and thereby satisfy their quick judgments or superficial understanding. I have found that not fitting in to a distinct societal cubical can be upsetting to those who need to fit everyone they meet into their personal worldview.

Traditionally speaking, I consider myself a *wikta*, a two-spirit. Two-spirit is a term coined in the late 1980s to early 1990s replacing the outdated term "berdache." "Berdache" is a blanket term used to try and categorize the many different genders each tribe had. This is different from being gay or transgender. Two-spirit means I have both a strong masculine spirit and a strong feminine spirit. My feminine side is drawn toward female fashion, dolls, and traditional female roles such as beading and skinning and butchering.

Wikta is a word for which there is no English equivalent. It breaks my heart to know that if I find what my people call *chante waste*, a good heart, or what English refers to as "love," that someone outside of my culture may not fully understand or accept it. This keeps me up at night. In the LDS religion, I am taught that a man and a woman complete each other. I wonder, if I already have both a male and female spirit inside me, then have I already completed my search for *chante waste*? Has my male and female already been joined? Is this part of my life already over before it begins? Or is there anyone out there for me?

I recall a particularly challenging day as I was sitting uncomfortably in a seminary class. I had had difficulties with this teacher before, but his words regarding my circumstances and confusion are etched in my memory.

"Homosexuality is a major cause of the moral decay of the family," his voice was feigning compassion. "And same-sex adoptions only add to that decay."

I shifted in my seat, hardly believing what I had just heard.

He went on to say, "If you accept the idea of homosexuals raising children—"

"You can't be serious," I interrupted, "at least these children are being offered a better life than they would have in the system."

He continued without acknowledging my point, "—if *you* accept the idea of homosexuality, then you sorely disagree with God."

I looked him in the eyes, trying not to show the tears welling up from my soul. My body acted on its own, standing up and walking out. By the end of the school day I was no longer enrolled in seminary. I was outed as "gay" to my bishop and those in my class. I found it strange that the following Sunday felt normal even though I couldn't look the bishop in the eye. I couldn't look myself in the eye.

Had I made a mountain out of a molehill? Had I been a drama queen? Was I just being extra? Through this experience, I developed a friendship with a very talented person at my school. She was in that seminary class and told me that ever since then she was inspired to speak out. She began to defend others and even wrote a three-page handwritten letter to the seminary teacher explaining why he should have a more tender heart on the subject, considering we are teenagers figuring out who we are. For the first time in my life, I felt as though someone had seen and acknowledged what I had done as a positive thing. While I don't hate the church, I do feel socially distanced from it. But I also recognize and appreciate all the many good people who belong to that group, including my mother.

I should admit that I have prayed to God to change me. It hasn't been easy to know who I am, but there is confidence knowing that this is the way He made me. This is the life God has given me. So my life is unsure. Instead of feeling like I have a plan of happiness, I feel that my plan includes dark clouds and a foggy future. Am I loveable? Can I have a family? Will I find peace? Can I find eternal happiness? Does my life moving forward include activity in the Church of Jesus Christ of Latter-day Saints, or will I look for happiness away from the gospel I was raised in?

I graduate from high school in a couple of months. My mother's house rule is that her children attend church with her until they graduate. Then we make our own decisions. I still don't know what my decision will be. I know I have a spiritual side that I need to tend to. Will I fill my spiritual needs through traditional worship? Where can I find a support group of spiritual friends that can share my burdens and strengthen me as I help shoulder their burdens? All I know for sure is that the uncertainty of my life requires me to rely on faith that things will get better, faith in a higher power, and faith that God and my mother love me. That faith leads to a hope that I can find a romantic someone who will love me for who I am and be willing to help me create a family on this earth, whatever that family looks like.

My people say *doksha* or "Creator Willing" as a way to align their will with God. My life is not over, and nothing is written in stone. Will I come to grips with accepting the church for what it is and accepting me for who I am? *Doksha.*

3

Frank Pellett's Story
Frank Pellett

My name is Frank Pellett. I'm a 44-year-old software developer for the LDS Church. I've sired 5 children and have been blissfully married for 16 years. I believe strongly in the church and the gospel, I'm recommend-holding, and glad to try whatever calling I'm given.

Two years ago, I also worked out that I am a transgender woman.

I say "worked out" because for most of my growing up, it never crossed my mind as possible. We were born the same gender we had been in the preexistence. It was a simple truth. Even though I did have many times where I wondered "what if," there wasn't any reason to question this truth. Three years ago, I learned about gender dysphoria, and it fit my life, the longing, like a glove. It took me another year to work out how being transgender could fit into LDS theology. I believe that gender is eternal, that I am the same gender I was in the preexistence, female, and for some reason(s) I have been sent to Earth in a body that was easily assigned male. I believe that in the next life my perfected body will reflect my spiritual gender.

Will I transition this body to presenting female? I don't know. I do know that when/if I do, it will be a decision between me, my wife, and God. It's not the business of anyone else.

How does my wife feel about this? She is supportive of me and wants to stay married to me (and I to her). We don't know what the status of our marriage will be in the next life. We just know that we want to be together forever. I figure if we need a male, we'll find someone we both can love.

And the church? Right now, not many people know. My bishop may know and hasn't said anything. Work doesn't know, and it's not something that comes up in conversation. I don't mind the information leaking out about my gender, but I'm not declaring it from the rooftops either. Both my wife and I strongly believe in the church and have no desire to leave it.

What about my sexual orientation? I am wholly attracted to women, and my wife in particular. She, however, is not attracted to women, but is attracted to me. It doesn't concern anyone other than us, since we plan to remain true to the covenants made when we married.

I am sure there are plenty of other questions, and I am always glad to answer them as they come. I'm not good at guile and don't like having things to hide. Being transgender is simply part of who I am. I don't yet have a "female" name, as I'm holding out hope my mother will give me one. My journey is certainly not representative of transgender women. The journeys of others are between them and God. I only hope that my journey can help others to see that we are here, as varied in our lives as any other people.

We are still your siblings, children of our Heavenly Parents.

On Hair and Intersections

Sarah Pace

4

I summoned up all my courage and walked into the hair salon. I had let my hair grow shaggy for a few months because my girlfriend likes it long, but I couldn't stand it touching my ears and getting in my eyes any more. The two stylists inside the salon appeared to be on their lunch break, chatting in Spanish with a TV playing in the background. I got the immediate sense that I had interrupted. I was about fifteen minutes early.

"Yes, can I help you?"

"Um, sorry. I have an appointment at 12:30?"

"Okay, yes. Sit down. She can help you."

I sat in the seat she indicated and listened as they continued their conversation. My unease grew. I hadn't realized this salon catered to Spanish-speaking clients. The Spanish that I learned while serving a stateside mission probably wouldn't be enough; I could barely understand their accents. At least they had spoken to me in English. Were they interpreting my skin color as Southeast Asian? Admittedly, my almond-shaped eyes were a little misleading.

"So how short do you want?"

"Um, mostly a trim. Well, it's been a while. I don't know. I like the sides shaved and the top cut so it sort of blends into it."

"A trim."

"Yeah, I guess. I mean, I kind of want a lot off."

"Ah. *Pelo de hombre.*"

Men's hair. A man's haircut. The plastic cape felt tight around my throat. *Don't react,* I told myself. Just like when the waiter calls me "Sir" or when the sweet visiting teacher comes over and thinks the rainbow flag on the wall means that I am an ally. It is easier to let people continue in their mistakes without embarrassing them through correction. For the rest of the haircut, I would just not let on that I understood her comment. Easy solution.

The clippers buzzed reassuringly against my head, while the bits of cut hair tickled my face. I tried to listen in on their conversation without reacting to any part of it. It was fairly easy to act like I didn't understand because the accent was so unfamiliar. Not as incomprehensible as the Cuban accents I occasionally heard on my mission, but close.

"So where are you from?" she began.

"California."

"Ah, *entonces hablas español.*"

"*Sí, más o menos.*"

Now I was stuck. Everything from here on out would be in Spanish. And she would know that I understood her comment about me wanting a men's haircut. I held tightly to the metal arms of the chair as the conversation slipped out of my control. Right on cue, the next question was,

"But your parents, where are they from?"

"Well, my mom is from Ecuador—"

The hum of the clippers suddenly stopped. I looked up at her reflection in the mirror, and she was staring back intensely.

"Really? Well then explain this to me: I know lots of Ecuadorian women and they all have long hair. Why do you have short hair?"

"Um, well, it's really thick and it gets hot in the summer," I mumbled.

"Oh. Okay then."

She looked back down at my head and continued cutting. My cheeks burned with embarrassment. I searched for the right term in my mind. Ah, yes: racial imposter syndrome. The feeling of discomfort that people (often those who are mixed-race) get when our actions or attributes do not meet expectations.

In this moment I felt the way I did as a freshman at BYU, having to fully confront my brown-skinned, white-washed, mixed-race reality. Back then, I felt insecure knowing that I appeared "exotic" but only spoke English, couldn't dance, and didn't know any traditional recipes. In fact, the sum of my knowledge about Ecuador came from an educational picture book about the Incas that I read as a child. The effects of interracial adoption had trickled down into the second generation, leaving me with obviously non-white features but none of the other expected traits to go along with them. The only thing that got me out of those months of racial discomfort was the dawning realization that I was gay and had eternity-related conundrums to ponder.

I bit the inside of my lip and tried to remind myself that my identity is valid. It is okay to be disconnected from my ethnic heritage. It is okay to like girls. It is okay to be brown and butch. It is okay.

I pushed my frustration away long enough to make small talk. She told me that she was Dominican and lived in the neighborhood nearby. She asked clarifying questions about how long I wanted my hair. I tried to communicate my vague opinions, cringing at my limited vocabulary.

The other woman answered a phone call and began arguing with her son on the other end. My stylist lapsed into silence, relieving me of my obligation to stumble through any more Spanish. I sank back into my anxious thoughts for a while.

"Wow, you are right. Your hair is very thick," she finally said.

"Haha, yeah, I know."

I was filled with relief and self-disgust. On the one hand, I had passed. Thick hair was enough of an excuse to have a short haircut, and my sexuality was not called into question. But still, why had I survived BYU and the church just to desperately stay in the closet?

"So what do you think?"

"It looks great. Thank you so much!" I lied.

I tipped heavily, hoping it would be enough to keep them from laughing about me the moment I walked out the door.

I didn't go to another salon. Instead, my hair was next cut by a friend, a coworker's partner, and then I even resorted to cutting it myself. Six months after the Imposter Syndrome Incident, I sat with my awkwardly shaggy hair on a chair inside my girlfriend's tiny bathroom.

The clippers were plugged in and balancing precariously on the window ledge. I had already prepped them by adding a few drops of oil to the blades, an action which always makes me think about priesthood blessings. A strange but practical anointing.

She turned on the music and began dividing my hair into sections. I gave a few basic instructions. The only other time she had cut it was about a year before, when we were both living in Provo. That time, she hadn't been satisfied with the end result and had vowed to never cut it again. Fortunately for me, she finally relented.

She laughed at the short ponytails sticking straight up on top of my head. We flirted. She leaned down and kissed me a couple times before the bits of hair covered everything. I worried slightly as the buzz of the clippers was punctuated with "Oops," and "Don't worry," and "I don't know where this part goes." But at least I was safe from uncomfortable salon small talk like, "Wow, does your whole family have such thick hair?" or "Do you have a boyfriend?" It gave me space to think about all the other various interactions I have had surrounding hair, race, sexuality, gender, and religion.

I thought about being misgendered in third grade and my first experience getting my eyebrows waxed as a teenager, finally feeling like I was succeeding at being female. I thought about going to a dating activity in my freshman ward and learning that men prefer women with long hair.

I remembered the MTC[1] president's wife demanding I get a haircut because my bangs were "covering my eyebrows and missionaries need their eyebrows visible so they can convey emotion."

A queer BYU friend whose hair I occasionally cut once said she didn't think of me as brown, and it hurt.

I remembered noticing when other short-haired girls on campus would make knowing eye contact with me and it made me feel special. Years later, I realized that they were probably gay, too, and maybe it was flirting. But they didn't intimidate or impress me as much as the group of tattooed, butch, Hispanic women I saw at Salt Lake Pride. Those women had filled me with a yearning to belong that was stronger than I had ever felt before.

My girlfriend finished shaving the sides and moved on to cutting the top layers with scissors. The hair fell onto my lap in two-inch long chunks. It felt freeing to watch the parts of myself that I had grown tired of simply fall away. It felt purifying.

I can't cut off any deeper parts of myself. Leaving the church didn't erase my years of complicated and often painful experiences there. The occasional times I've attended church I haven't felt the sense of peace I used to find when I was younger. Living in either white space or brown space doesn't cure my feeling of somehow being an outsider. There is no easy way to escape the discomfort of my conflicting identities. There is no way to choose one and let go of the others, because how could I choose?

NOTE

1. MTC stands for "Missionary Training Center." Future missionaries attend the MTC for a brief period of time prior to going on their missions. They learn the language they are going to be speaking and they are trained in how to be a missionary.

5

I Give You a Name (& This Is My Blessing)

Aisling "Ash" Rowan

Lights shone down onto the concrete stage, music chirped to life, and all—except one—of the tutu-adorned toddlers began their ungraceful dance.

In full view of a captive audience of beaming adults, I plopped myself belly-down onto the floor. My round face rested in my cupped hands as I kicked one leg and then the other, back and forth, and watched the rest of my class perform.

This nonconformity was no isolated incident. In kindergarten, I went through a phase of signing all my papers as "Robert." (I don't remember why; I don't feel like a Robert.) Soon after, I fell in love with the idea of a character like Disney's version of Mulan, who faced the role that had been chosen for her and replied with every one of her actions: *no thanks*. And as a vainglorious adolescent, with a kind of pluck I seem to have since misplaced, I enlisted all my friends—and several long-suffering teachers—in referring to me, exclusively, as Platypus.

As I'm typing these anecdotes out, in my cobbled-together "working from home" area, it's easy to play office-chair psychologist. And I'm horrified to see now how much I didn't know then. At the time, I could only perceive myself and my world as if through a mirror, darkly.

And that's because I still had Something to meet.

My siblings and I adored PBS shows, and one late afternoon when our cartoons rolled into the adult stuff, nobody felt motivated to go turn the TV off. So, the narrator of NOVA went on uninterrupted while explaining the science of sex—a word I still blushed to hear, even though in this context I knew it didn't mean reproduction.

I should change the channel, I thought—this seemed like something I shouldn't be watching.

But I stalled.

Something lingered there with me, looking on in rapt and silent interest.

The program went on, detailing the lives of some people who were "transgender," which apparently meant that they changed their bodies to try and be the other sex. To my young mind, they ended up . . . just looking somewhat off, like someone in a costume. And now, out of a fascinated revulsion, I couldn't look away.

When Mom came in to say our screen time was up, I startled and tried to scramble for the remote—but she only frowned at the TV with genuine sympathy.

"Those people are confused," she said sadly. (You had to be, right? To do something so drastic?)

But luckily, transgender people are a rare anomaly.

And as I wandered out of the room, I reassured myself that I didn't really need to stress over something so abstract and far away.

At my twelfth birthday party, in our family living room, the other kids all circled up around me. They chattered with excitement as I eagerly reached for the next gift. My fingers fumbled with the wrapping paper before revealing a small, zippered bag.

"Oohh!" I grinned at its beachy vinyl print. "Super cute pencil pouch! Thank you."

"It's a *purse*," corrected the gift-giver immediately, as if it should have been obvious. Maybe it was to everyone else.

Then she scoffed. "What kind of *girl are* you?"

Inside, I yelled. *I'm not like you! I'm no good at being a girl, and I never will be! I don't get it! I don't know what's wrong with me! I'm doing it wrong!*

I set the purse down to the side, swallowed back my anger, and forced a smile before replying. "I'm just a weird one, I guess."

The Something stirred and grumbled softly but had nothing more to say.

Seated on the floor of my brother's room, I rolled his pocketknife idly in my palm. He and my parents had heard—many, many times—my thoughts on the matter. They'd seen my glower as he selected it off the shelf.

"Girls can have pocketknives, too," I muttered.

As far as I could tell, no good reason kept us from copying the "cooler" boys' activities, like knots and car repairs, and going on treks and hikes and campout adventures. To be fair, I did also enjoy learning to knead warm dough in our leader's kitchen; cutting and pasting patterned paper shapes; and yes, even trying on outfits at Kohl's for a cheesy "modesty fashion show." I liked *most* of our activities, but I still wanted *all* of it. Not just the half I'd been shoved into, for . . . some reason.

It seemed as if everyone around me had a silent agreement about arbitrary Rules like this, and I hadn't been informed or consulted.

Girls like clothes and scrapbooks, the Rules say. *Boys like camping and hiking.*

"And what about *me*?" I wanted to say. "I like *all* of it."

But Rules are Rules. *You are a "girl." Your best friend is a "boy." So everyone on the bus and playground—even your 6th grade teacher—will insist you're "in love." On Tuesday nights, your friend will be dragged to the other side of the church while you trail behind the young women like a dog with its tail tucked.*

And, the Rules go on, *when girls go to church, they dress up nice and do their hair. They wear dresses and skirts—only those. Pants are not allowed.*

No pants, and no matter how dapper you think they look, absolutely no bow ties.

That jolted me back to my senses. Mom had just told us something about one of our cousins going through a phase of exploration, and how disappointing it was that our aunt encouraged it—wearing ties and all.

"She's confused," Mom had said, shaking her head. "Heavenly Father made us a certain way."

My fingers curled tightly around the pocketknife. The Something fluttered back to life in my chest, but all it could do was breathe heavily. We both knew Mom was right.

And yet the world wouldn't end if I put on a bow tie. But why was I the only one who wanted to? What was wrong with me?

All the girls around me seemed to excel at following the Rules. I only seemed to excel at lying on the stage when someone told me to perform.

My splotchy-faced reflection glared at me when I glanced at the mirror, so I pouted elsewhere while Mom reached for another strand of my hair to style. She brought the steaming curling rod startlingly close to my neck, and I instinctively winced away.

Boys don't have to do this. It hurts! And it's not, well, me. *That isn't me.*

A little wide-eyed, I peered into the mirror again. The makeup looked objectively nice. And like Mom had pointed out, makeup is basically drawing and painting on your face, and I do love art!

But seeing it on my own face, framed by golden spirals of long hair, made my stomach lurch. It felt the same as hearing two discordant notes being played together. It looked like someone doing their best to masquerade as a pretty girl—but still, always, coming up just a little short.

The Something lifted its head and gave a low, long, mournful bellow.

I know, I agreed, softly, cringing at another curl being tugged.

It hurts.

One weird thing about years is that they can seem to pass quicker than the days that comprise them. In a whirlwind of research papers and exams, falling in love while cleaning toilets, and a thunderstorm-maelstrom of an engagement, all at once I'd graduated with a degree from BYU in illustration plus one cute dork of a spouse. We'd even managed to make two little sprogs of our own, but as it turns out, raising young offspring is no easy feat.

Tearful and aimless after another grueling evening, I wandered into the front room. It welcomed me in with its dark expanse and deafening quiet—something that had become totally foreign, and starkly contrasted with our rowdy daytimes.

As usual, I couldn't sleep. Even while my body slowed and begged for rest, my mind continued to spin and whirl.

Earlier that day, the Spouse and I had watched an episode of *Adam Ruins Everything,* in which a character named Rhea shows up to give Adam some playful sibling grief. The Something perked up as I realized, with delight, that I couldn't tell if this was meant to be Adam's sister? Brother? Sister? *Sibling?*

A scramble over to IMDb showed that Rhea Butcher—who has since come out as nonbinary—also did stand-up, as well as co-starring in a series with fellow comic (and wife) Cameron Esposito. Another win for the queer-radar.

Some slice-of-life queer comedy/romance sounded like exactly the light and fluffy antidote my heart needed, so I hit "play" on the first episode of *Take My Wife.* And soon enough, I couldn't stop smiling.

The "me" of not so long ago could never have imagined *choosing* something like this, let alone finding so much solace in it. But six years of being on Tumblr, and the Internet at large, had gradually changed my perception and understanding of being queer. I'd been introduced to a vibrant community of individuals, far different from the shameful myths I'd accumulated over a lifetime. Part of me even began to identify along with them when I discovered the term *asexual* sometime in the early 2010s (though that will have to wait for another essay).

I'd been the most wrong about trans people. The more I learned, the more I loved. I found myself coming back to a particular subreddit that documents transitions, and I'd beam over the before-and-after photo comparisons. You can't help but cheer someone on when you see how their whole persona has brightened, with confidence and contentment glimmering in their eyes. It's a blessing to witness someone blooming into the person they were always meant to become.

And it also filled me with longing. I kept returning to these transition stories, the YouTube journeys of people like Ash Hardell, and the Something would always be right there, whining and groaning because I so badly wanted that to be me.

If only.

One spring afternoon, in a recliner in a chapel's mothers' lounge, I scrolled through Tumblr on my phone while my son nursed. A post about gender identities popped up on the screen, a few paragraphs about various experiences that I absolutely resonated with. Things I had felt for as long as I could remember, even before I had enough words or awareness to notice. And at long last, Something—I almost physically felt it—clicked into place.

"I think I'm nonbinary," I thought placidly, as I tapped to reblog the post. Then I looked up at the Something.

The Something stared, unblinking, back at me.

*

My prayers have never felt right as a formal affair. The most meaningful discussion I've ever had with God happened in two words and a feeling, tucked into bed in a pitch-black hotel room. The air conditioner whirred like sacred droning, and with sudden insistence, Something in me coalesced to proclaim:

I'm trans!

A warmth of assurance spread through my entire figure, like sunlight spilling to fill a room. It felt good. And every time I think back on it, the same phrase comes to me: *I know it, and I know God knows it, and I cannot deny it.*

Then, just as quickly, a shadow crept into my gut.

"This must be a warning, right?" I asked the ceiling. "You're only telling me this so clearly because I'm gonna need to *really* know it. Something's going down tomorrow."

With a frown, and then a small nod to myself, I burrowed under the covers and slipped into uneasy dreaming.

Content note: The next section contains direct quotes from a conference address by Dallin H. Oaks.[1]

All throughout the next morning's session of General Conference,[2] I fidgeted atop the disheveled bedsheets—and not just because Elder Cook had dropped a bombshell about church services transitioning to a two-hour block. Every word buzzed right by me, as if the TV were broadcasting static instead of prophetic counsel.

The final speaker took his place. My stomach lurched.

As Elder Oaks's face appeared on-screen, the Something charged into the room and bared its teeth.

"Gender is eternal," Elder Oaks said directly to me, with his usual grim finality—like a judge delivering a sentence. "We *all* lived as male or female spirits in the presence of God."

I desperately wished that static would save me now, but every sonorous statement ("suffer from self-inflicted spiritual blindness") sent a shuddering shockwave through my skull ("put their eternal soul at risk") until I couldn't tell which beat harder—the apostle's declarations, or my own racing heart.

I need to run. I felt the flight instinct viscerally, and yet I couldn't tear myself away, as if my nerves had stopped taking any advice from upstairs. And so I stared. And listened. And trembled.

The moment he finally stopped talking, I raced into the bathroom and collapsed, heaving, in front of the toilet. The cheery sounds of the Tabernacle Choir echoed distantly behind me.

But I'm trans! I thought, putting clammy hands to cold porcelain. *You told me I'm nonbinary, and that felt so right and good. How can one of Your servants—one of Your prophets!—say otherwise?*

No answer came. Beneath the ringing in my ears, I thought back to that instant of clarity, and realized I'd been given a choice. Which voice would I listen to—the one that made me feel like this?

Still shaking, I met my own green-tinged gaze in the steely mirror.

Or, would I hold tight to that halcyon whisper in the eye of a hurricane?

Through the courthouse's large windows, muted sunlight pours over the floor. I breathe in deeply, and walk forward with purpose and a smile. My chest fills with a bright certainty and, looking down on the traffic flowing down a snowy State Street, I'm reminded of the early years when I called this city home.

This is for you, I think. *Little me.*

I'm also wearing a Doctor Who patterned bow tie, and I look pretty damn great.

A few minutes before the hearing is due to start, I enter the courtroom and take my seat quietly, still unsure of what to expect.

Firstly, I'd imagined someone austere, but the judge who enters the room—while he definitely has a commanding presence—speaks kindly, and with warmth. He asks us all to be seated, then asks if the name listed before him is the right one. I'm prepared to fight tooth and nail for it, but moments after my affirmation, His Honor is already signing his own name at the end of my petition.

The whole thing has taken maybe three minutes. I blink.

That's it?

The gentle judge congratulates me and leaves me alone with the court clerks, who finish their important-sounding typing and then direct me downstairs.

Downstairs, to get the official paperwork documenting my new name.

My name! The name that fits me, that I chose and I get to be called by. My parents aren't with me—and it feels like they should be, though I hadn't even told them this would happen—but as my chest expands with a joy I can't contain, I know my Heavenly Parents are looking on, proudly.

"And *you*!" Coming back out into the hallway, I stand before the Something that has been with me all these years. It quirks its head sideways.

"I name you, too," I say. "You were my shame and my fear. You wanted to keep me safe, so you followed me and questioned me—made me question—and I still made it this far. With you, and in spite of you.

"Somehow, though, you've become something else. You've matured right along with me. And now, I call you Resilience. The marker of where I started, but more importantly—proof of who I'm becoming. In those moments where I once felt shame, I'll now choose delight. I choose bravery, admiration, and compassion. I choose to become myself, and the way that God wants me to be. I hear Their voice, and I act on it."

I look down at the pages I hold, grinning.

"And the name by which I will be known is Ash Rowan."

NOTES

1. Dallin H. Oaks is a member of the quorum of the twelve apostles of the Church of Jesus Christ of Latter-day Saints. Apostles are sometimes called by the title "Elder," as are missionaries. Dallin H. Oaks is known for anti-queer rhetoric, and suicide help lines are often put up in queer Mormon support groups when he is scheduled to speak. Content warnings often accompany his name in queer Mormon spaces.

2. General Conference is a twice annual conference held by the LDS Church. Members attend world-wide via broadcast and speakers typically include general authorities and general officers.

6

Immersive Theater
Jenn Lee Smith

One wintry day in Provo, Utah, my friend and I braved the gelid roads on foot to visit a tall, good-looking boy she liked who lived south of campus. We were chatting with his roommates when he walked in and introduced himself to her.

"Hi, I'm Scott," he said, holding his hand out to be shaken.

I looked from him to her and back again, completely confused. He'd seen her many times to the point of being her date to winter formal just last week. They had dinner together and danced all night. I was there.

"Yeah, I know," my friend said as she haltingly held out her hand to meet his. I've always been impressed by her patience and levelheadedness.

"Huh," he responded and turned to me asking, "And you are?"

I felt that familiar cringe and decided to laugh it off saying, "I *was not* your date last week in Salt Lake—she was."

My friend quickly diffused the situation saying, "It's fine, all Asians look alike."

His face relaxed, signaling to all that it is, indeed, fine. We laughed, the white boys and us. That's what two Asian women do at Brigham Young University in situations like this. We move on and pretend racially insensitive things don't happen. Our jokes are white-people-friendly. We gloss over the culture, teachings from prophets, and the very scripture that point to a racially hierarchical view of the world. Back then, over 95% of the students at BYU had European ancestry. I learned that it was never okay to bring up that fact, and to always make sure they felt comfortable around me, the foreigner. I rattled off scripted answers they wanted to hear when asked, "Where are you *really* from and why is your English so good?"

If I stuck to the script, they would have fewer reasons to assault or humiliate me (a story for another time). I was more likely to be safe from harm and rejection if I conceded that my particular color assigned me to a role of passivity. More importantly, I would be validated and I would belong in this world of white Mormons, even if it was at the high, existential cost of my dignity and value.

"When I see you and talk to you, I don't see color or think of you as not white," was a comment I heard a lot. Safety and invisibility achievement unlocked.

Back then, my attraction to women was also safely hidden, especially from myself. It was revealed later, after marriage to a man. Now as a straight-passing woman, I am more aware of the intersection of my multiple marginalities and how they compound my invisibility in many of the spaces I move through. I am not entirely sure of what the path is toward queer visibility. This is the dilemma of discovering one's queerness after a temple marriage and kids. When I felt that powerful, chemical attraction to a woman, my immediate reaction was resistance: this is not my story. This is too much to add to a highly sensitive body already wrestling with childhood, developmental, race, ethnic, immigration, and religious abuses and traumas.

Sometime later, I signed up for a free immersive theater experience, called *Red Flags,* without fully knowing what it was. I was traveling for work and it seemed like a fun idea. And it was free. I just had to wait to receive a text from a fake blind date fifteen minutes before the assigned time. When I got the text, it was from a woman named Emily. I felt myself freeze: Is that what *immersive* theater means? Rising panic eventually gave way to the realization that I was in a city where I knew no one, so, why not try?

I showed up at our appointed time and waited near the bar. And waited. At last, a cute, quirky, wide-eyed woman appeared before me.

"I am so sorry. I had to take my dog to the vet, which was close to this coffee shop with a pastry I like so I had to stop for that," she said with feigned sincerity.

"Um, no worries, must be great pastry, sorry about your dog," I blurted out feeling the anxiety rising as my eyes darted around the room full of people chatting with drinks in hand.

The actress, in character, took my response as an invitation to talk another ten minutes about her dog, which allowed me time to lean into the reality and excitement of being on a date with a woman.

I was enjoying every mundane, comedic detail about their trip to the vet when Emily paused and said, "I've been rambling this whole time. Tell me about you."

As I began a made-up story of my own that was pretty close to the truth, she picked up her phone and started to text.

"Just a sec." She put one finger up while typing away. "I'm telling my friend about the vet."

"I am so impressed with how much you care about your dog—that is such an attractive quality," I said, now fully invested in my own character as someone who is unfazed by red flags.

"Really? Normally around this time my dates say they never want to see me again."

"I don't know why they'd say that. I'm having a really good time." And I was.

She put her hand on my hand and sat closer to me. From head to toe I felt warmth like from a soft blanket. No one was paying any heed and even if they did, the growing calm and solidity inside my body seemed to matter more in that moment than anything that was happening around us. My normally shaky sense of self came into focus for a few brief seconds.

"Do you want to kiss?" she asked, leaning in.

There was a space of quiet that lasted a breath, long enough to realize that I hadn't resisted or fought the invitation of the last hour and that this question, meant for humor and fun, was now too serious for me. I mumbled something as I backed away and flew out of the room into the night.

Later that evening, we spotted each other at a gathering where I apologized for breaking character and explained that I had grown up in a highly demanding, heteronormative religion. (I probably said I was Mormon and no further explanation was needed.) Her eyes lit up. She knew something about that and not just because she was also raised in a religion with similar demands (Judaism), but because her Mormon cousin came out as lesbian a few years back after marrying a man.

As I stood speechless, she added, "I didn't know there were Asian Mormons!"

I laughed and we hugged as I replied, "I didn't know Mormons had Jewish cousins!"

All of me came together for that brief moment. We saw each other, appreciated our differences, and I thought, so this is what visibility feels like.

My Agender, Autistic Mormon Life

Mette Harrison

7

I was diagnosed with autism at the age of forty-six, in 2017. A lot of people ask me why I bothered. I have a relatively successful life, am married to a man and have been a parent to five wonderful children. But I kept tripping over autism. Friends had kids being diagnosed with it. Family members had children who were diagnosed with it. And the descriptions of the traits sounded so familiar. But also, I had come to a place in my life where I wanted to know what was wrong with me. The answer was, in many ways, autism.

I don't mean to say that I think autism answers all of my questions about myself and why I do the things that I do. I also don't mean to say that I believe I'm a crappy, worthless human because I'm autistic and I wish I wasn't (though those feelings have been a constant problem since my diagnosis). I just mean that, as I hit my forties, I think I hit that stage of life where you start to go inward. You begin to ask if what you've been told your whole life is really true—about the world and about yourself. You begin to reconsider what makes people good humans, what is human in the first place, what is good. You try to look at yourself in a new light, to accept your flaws and to see the whole story of yourself.

For me, that story had to include autism. As a storymaker, autism was necessary in order to see myself truly, all the parts of me. And maybe even as an autist, it was important for me to place this last brick in the wall of my new building front so that I could make new lists to sort myself into, new rules for how to be a better human. That is, I suppose, my deeper quest: how to be a better human. Sometimes the answers to that are to be more autistic. Sometimes they are to let go of my clinging to this or that and to step away from the autism that is so natural to me, to embrace a scary world of otherness (that's you guys, neurotypical types).

I've never felt quite female. This is part of my autistic story. Autistic people are about four times more likely to identify as trans than the rest of the population. I don't think of myself as trans, but gender is very tricky for me. I've struggled with it all my life, with the expectations of what girls are like, what they are allowed to do, what they are supposed to become as women. Though adults are often telling children that they are too immature to say what their sexual identity is or what their gender identity is, I knew as young as eight that I wasn't like other girls.

Some days I liked girl clothes, but not often. I especially disliked the color pink, any ruffles, or feminine details. I can't tell anymore if this was internalized misogyny or if it was something else. I liked physical activity and I didn't like that girls' clothing seemed to interfere with that. I hated it when people told me what girls could or couldn't do.

"Ladies don't chew gum," my mother would tell me.

"Ladies don't show their underwear," she would say when I did somersaults or climbed trees or did the monkey bars.

But why? I might have been a budding feminist, but mostly I just thought the "rules" of gender were stupid and nonsensical.

Why wasn't I supposed to like competitive sports? Why was I not supposed to be good at math and science? Why was I supposed to let boys talk instead of answering questions when I knew better than they did? Why did I have to be nice? Why did I have to say yes to boys all the time? Why did I have to wait for boys to ask me on dates?

I tried being a boy for a while when my mom cut my hair too short. She wasn't great with scissors in the first place, and I was probably wiggly. She kept cutting it shorter and shorter until it was boy-length.

"You'll like it that way for the summer," she said. "It will be lighter and easier to take care of."

She was right about that, but I liked it for other reasons, too. Teachers at school the next year (my hair still very short) thought I was a boy in my "sturdy" cords and the striped T-shirts I found in the boys' section at Sears, which my mother approved of because they would "wash well." I found that teachers and students treated me differently. Teachers let me answer questions more often, gave me more freedom in general. Other students let me be more aggressive on the playground.

This could be a typical trans story except that I didn't like being a boy any more than I liked being a girl. Being a boy had a set of other weird rules about gender. Boys weren't allowed to cry or touch each other in comfort. They couldn't do anything deemed "feminine"—even something as ordinary as a game of jacks on the playground led to me being mocked and teased for being a "girl."

These things all led me to go back to being a girl at school and at home simply because I grew breasts and it was more difficult to switch back and forth between genders. By the time I was in high school, it felt like the rules of being a girl were a heavy burden to bear. It was a complicated combination of autism and gender. I hated having breasts most of the time, simply because they were annoying. I didn't like wearing clothes that showed off my body because I was self-conscious about my visible femininity. In Mormonism, this was often coded as me being properly "modest," even though it was really something else completely.

Looking back, I think most of high school was another kind of masquerade, this one of being a woman. I wore makeup most of the time, except when I was simply too tired and couldn't stand it anymore. Then I went to school in sweats and I cut my hair short again. I dated young men and was envious of them at times, and then equally pitying of them for all the same reasons that I had seen in elementary school. Men and women were wearing different straitjackets, but they were straitjackets all the same. Why?

When I went to grad school and studied feminist theories, I began to spout ideas that men and women were not essentially different in any of the ways that Mormonism insisted they were. This was my own experience in the world because I'd been able to pass as male and as female, and it all felt like just nonsense to me, like gender had nothing to do with my essential self. But I also learned that you can't inhabit this world unless you pick one of two genders. Sometimes it feels like saying *agender* or *nonbinary* or any of the other words that try to be outside of the binary is just another way of admitting that the binary is the primary way that everyone accepts they must be. And again, I ask why?

I understand that I am seen as female by anyone who looks at me and it's easier to accept female titles socially for someone who is already extremely socially awkward. I don't do polite conversation. If you talk to me, we're going to go straight to the deep stuff. I don't have time for the weather and I'm certainly not interested in talking about shopping or the latest, most popular TV shows. I have no FOMO: I'm never afraid to miss out on anything. And that also means I struggle with jokes because I don't have the same reference points the rest of you have. I haven't attended church for over a year, and that means I have a lot of dresses in my closet that

I don't wear anymore because my go-to wardrobe is a sports bra, race T-shirt, and jeans. Because it's masculine? No, because it's comfortable and because race T-shirts allow me to parade my competitive side around. Why should it be seen as masculine for me to enjoy passing guys with much bigger bikes (and muscles) on my tiny, little red Cervélo? It's just me.

I went out bra shopping with my daughters recently and I remember the saleswoman tried to convince me that I'd look "great" in a padded bra.

"Do you have anything that makes my boobs look smaller?" I asked.

She gave me the strangest look. "Normally, women want to accentuate their figures," she tried to explain to me, the autistic, agender weirdo in front of her.

Normally, perhaps they do. I am not normal.

I see the ways in which I have been trained to act as a woman in conversations, to let men take the lead, to demur. I have many good female friends, but I have also found that they are less feminine than most, and not surprisingly, are also sometimes autistic themselves, or autistic adjacent. Yet I often find I connect with men, who tend to be more blunt and circumlocute less than women do.

Is this because of autism? Or because of my gender issues? I don't know and at some point it's probably not useful to try to disentangle those identities. Gender is just a thing other people believe about me, not the way I think or feel about myself. In a way, playing the game of being a woman is almost protective, because I can keep my secret self hidden and not visible to other people who might see me truly and think me too strange for comfort.

Call me what label you choose. It doesn't matter to me. I'm not listening. I'm too busy with this project of figuring out more about myself as I shed the layers of what other people have told me I must be.

Married and Bisexual

Amber Lewis

8

My husband and I went to a movie theater to see *Big Hero 6* for our first date, and movies have kind of been our thing ever since. So, of course, I saw the movie *Bohemian Rhapsody*, alongside my husband and brother. I, however, never could have imagined the impact watching *Bohemian Rhapsody*, especially alongside my brother and husband, would have on me.

After the movie, my husband and I went to dinner and then went home. Our conversation centered almost entirely on *Bohemian Rhapsody*. I tried my best to be as normal as I could be, hoping to prevent my husband from knowing my true feelings. But when our conversation seemed to lull, the words just flew out.

"Do you love me?" I asked in a meek voice. My husband seemed to sense something was going on.

"Yeah, do you love me?" he answered, his voice not quite as enthusiastic as usual.

"Yeah," I replied quickly. And then the silence began to creep back in. My husband continued to drive, and we put a few more miles behind us.

"I think there's something I need to tell you," I said in a slow voice. It felt like molasses flowing out of my mouth, hot and thick.

"Okay . . ." he responded, almost as slowly as I did.

"Have you ever heard of the Kinsey scale?" I inquired with a twinge of confidence, as I was sure he hadn't.

"No," he replied quickly.

"It's named after the man who created it. He did some research on people and how heterosexual and how homosexual people are. He figured out a lot of people aren't truly heterosexual or homosexual—a lot of people are actually somewhere in between." I paused slightly to look at his reaction. It didn't appear he had figured it out.

"It's on a scale of zero to six—don't ask me why that's how it's set up, it's just what Kinsey decided. Zero means someone is 100% heterosexual, and six means someone is 100% homosexual, and," I had never said it before. I held my breath, but not by choice; I couldn't breathe.

"And I'm not a zero."

Sixth, seventh, and eighth grade were not kind to me. What I understand now is that I was struggling with undiagnosed major depressive disorder, but all I knew then was I was in constant mental and emotional pain, yet somehow felt numb. I was so numb, in fact, that I have very few memories from this time. I have more memories of fifth grade than eighth grade, even though eighth grade is more recent.

It seems more like a memory than a dream, but I can still feel that moment. I was at school. It was sixth grade. She was in at least one of my classes all year long. She was tall and curvy with long caramel-brown hair. Her eyes were dark, cool brown. She had a sweet laugh and was very smart, and she was so beautiful. Over the course of that year, she and I became friends. I always wanted to talk to her. I always wanted to sit by her. I always wanted to sit by her.

I began to have questions. There was a boy that I knew I had a crush on, but surely this couldn't be the same thing. He had blond hair, she had brown. He had glasses, she did not. But they were both in the orchestra. And they were both very smart. But he was a boy. Girls don't like girls. Every time the possibility that I saw her as anything more than a friend entered my head, I shook my head and pushed it out. I didn't like her like that; she was just nice, which made her a good friend. And anyone who knew anything about American beauty standards could look at her and see that she was beautiful. She was just a friend. She was just a friend. She was just a friend.

I didn't move. I loved him, but the only thing running through my mind was the scene in *Bohemian Rhapsody* when Freddie told Mary he was bisexual, and Mary gave back her engagement ring.

"So, are you saying you like girls?" my husband asked timidly. I just continued to sit there in silence. What would he do?

"Yes. I think so," I finally answered. Sheer panic. "I think I'm a one on the Kinsey scale. I like girls, but I definitely like boys more," I quickly added, with a definite sense of rushed urgency in my voice. However, there was only more silence.

"Amber, it's okay. You think you're a one? I think a lot of people out there are ones. I'm always going to love you."

What made me think I could handle taking eighteen college credits when I have multiple health problems is beyond me. If I was awake, I was doing homework, and doing this while living with my in-laws in a house that held seven other people put me under a level of stress that I didn't know existed.

It started at midterms. Night after night, I dreamt of girls. Some that I knew or knew of, others seemed to be strangers. What they had in common is that they were lovely. And for the first time in my life, it felt like I experienced the forbidden touch. In my sleep, I felt alive, but when I woke up I was left feeling confused. Why was I having dreams like this? Why now?

With the dreams came memories. Girls who were beautiful and sweet and kind, girls who made great friends. Finally, after years, I allowed the idea into my mind: I might be bisexual. But what I didn't know is that, once I allowed myself to think the thought for the very first time, it would grow roots and sprout like a tree.

My mom has been an active participant in multiple LDS LGBTQ groups for years. My brother is gay, and my mother began trying her best to discover what she can do to help her child. By now, I had been aware that I am bisexual for about six months. My husband had been more than accepting; he had questions like, "I look at Chris Evans and I can see that he's an attractive man, but I'm not attracted to him. What do you experience?" However, I had not told anyone other than my husband that I am bisexual. You would think that, having a gay brother who was accepted for being gay, I would have no problem telling my mom that I'm bisexual, but for some reason I just didn't.

I wasn't shocked when my mom invited me to the Affirmation Conference[1] in June of 2019. That seemed fun; I loved being an ally of the LGBTQ community, and I could easily pass myself off as such without my mom finding out that I'm actually a member of the community. I drove down to Provo and met up with my mom on the first day of the conference, and we met up with my gay brother at the conference. The first thing we attended was the first-timers meeting. As it turned out, we ended up sitting right behind a couple my mom had met through Mama Dragons,[2] and they began chatting about their children after the meeting. My brother decided to walk around, and it suddenly hit me: tell him. Again, the words just fell out. No thought, it just happened.

"So, we're friends, right?" I blurted out, surprising myself as much as I did him.

"Umm. Yeah. What's up?" he responded with that same twang of concern.

"I'm bisexual," I said brazenly. His face showed it all. His eyebrows rose and he half nodded.

"Oh. Okay," he answered with thinly veiled surprise. We continued to walk, and about five minutes later, he asked flatly, "So where are you on the Kinsey scale?"

"Like a one."

"So you lean more to guys than girls but still like girls."

"Pretty much."

"Okay."

And that was that.

The next day, my mom and I attended a breakout session for allies. Everyone in the session was broken up into groups to have undirected discussions about the LGBTQ community and how we could help them. Most of the participants in the group were parents of an LGBTQ child. Two of the participants in my group included a mother of a gay son and bisexual daughter, and a mother of a transgender child. Hearing the mother of the gay and bisexual children speak for some reason gave me courage; apparently this is a thing that happens. As for the mother of a transgender child, she was so pure and so kind. I had to talk to her. I had to talk to my mom, and I had to talk to this mom because my heart was in my throat.

Once the session ended, my mom and I left the room, and my mom left to go to the bathroom. Bingo. I watched her walk down the stairs, and then darted back into the room. The mom was still there. She saw me approaching her, and she gave me a hug. For reasons I still don't understand, I laid everything out to this woman I had met an hour earlier. I have no idea why this seemed so important to me, but it did.

"Well, you know your mom. But I heard her while she was here, and it may take her some time, but I'm sure she'll love you no matter what." And it was at this moment my mom walked in. We said our goodbyes, and my mom and I went to the next session. After that session, my mom drove me back to the hotel to get my things and car so I could go to a bridal shower back home (it was actually a bachelorette party where we learned how to pole dance, but she wasn't ready to hear that). We were driving when she brought up a mutual friend who is bisexual, and I knew it was now or never.

"Speaking of bisexuals, I have something I've been thinking about telling you the last two days, and that's why I went back after the ally session—I'm bisexual." Silence. Nothing.

"Does your husband know?" she finally managed to timidly push out.

"Yeah, and he's fine with it." More silence.

"How long have you known?"

"I think I've known since I was twelve, but I shoved it into a deep, dark hole, and it kind of slipped out." There was no silence this time.

"How did that happen? You're married. You've made a commitment," she stammered out quickly.

"I don't know. I was stressed during the Fall semester of last year, and for some reason it just kind of came up."

"Okay, because you're the one who chose to get married, and you chose to stand by your husband."

"Yes, and I was bisexual when I got married."

The next week consisted of me getting a text almost once a day, either about "you made a commitment" or "nothing good will come out of you telling people, so don't." I began to feel uncomfortable around my mom because I didn't want to hear more of her word-vomiting while brazenly ignoring my attempts to explain that all the things she was worried about weren't worth being worried about. I chose to stay at my parents' house on the 4th of July because I figured there would be less fireworks, and I was on edge the whole day. As I was going to bed, I snapped. I was sick of this.

It was a late night. I remember few specifics; mostly I remember my mom insisting she was just trying to help, and me trying to insist she was being biphobic and not listening when I did try to talk to her. My dad got involved. It's his words I remember most: "It is done. Everyone who needs to know knows. It's not an issue unless we make it an issue. So let's just let it be and not talk about it again."

And that was that. The whole problem was wrapped with a bow. My mom never accused me of being promiscuous again, and I didn't get after my mom again. The expectation of silence was put in place. The expectation is for me to never tell anyone, ever. I can never be out publicly; it'll hurt my brother, husband, and future children. There's enough bi activists already and I don't need that "negative attention," apparently. And so here I continue to sit, in silence, just like I did when I was twelve. I will never dispel any myths, I will never be an example to other young bisexuals, I will never be able to show that families can have more than one LGBTQ person in them. So in silence I sit.

NOTES

1. Affirmation (affirmation.org) is an organization that provides support for LGBTQ Mormons and their family/friends. They have an annual international conference, typically held in Utah.

2. Mama Dragons is a nonprofit organization that supports the parents of queer Mormons.

9

The Silence That Echoes

Melissa Malcolm King

Once, in Salt Lake City, I boarded a train intending to march with my rainbow family.

As I tried to exit the train, a man standing with a group of other men called out, "Hey, N——!"

Flashback to childhood in Long Island. We'd moved into a white neighborhood. N-word and swastikas all over the house.

I wanted to run. And then I wanted to fight, but then I knew the police would side with him. I could run or I could fight but either way I was going to lose.

I moved further away from him, trying desperately to find the emergency call button. Why wouldn't the door open?

The group of men followed me. One of them yelled in a scruffy voice, "Go back to Africa."

I didn't look up, but glanced quickly and saw his angry eyes, looking out at the rainbow march.

"Between the homos and the n——, I don't know which one is worse," he stated flatly.

I looked around. There were at least fifteen people in the car. They would glance up and then quickly look down at their phones. One woman holding tightly to the hand of a young child moved away. I felt like I was in a warzone but I was being seized as the only soldier surrounded by enemies.

It was not the words I was called but the echo of silence that pierced my soul.

After this incident I didn't have the energy to march alongside my rainbow family. I felt my courage to march and to be who I am, it was stripped away. I felt weak, like a wounded bird. This all took place at the intersection of the temple, the rainbow march, and where I live near Temple Square. I'm literally stuck in these intersections all the time: between the church, my sexual/gender orientation, and a society that normalizes racism. I'm at the intersection of all these places that I want to call home, but they are connected by disjointed bridges.

As a queer, disabled, multiracial person of color the message is loud and clear: you are not worthy and you are not wanted here. In other words, get straight, get white, don't fight, and then you'll be alright.

I am not trying to flaunt my homosexuality, gender identity, and the expressions that come with them. I am simply showing pride in who I am and who God made me to be.

I am tired of being a second-class citizen. I am tired of burying my friends who have died by suicide. I am tired of wiping aside tears where joy should abound.

I want to give hope to those who are silently suffering so that they will have the strength to live another day. I am looking to have a spiritual life. I fight to be visible in this community while most world religions have deemed the LGBTQ community to be unworthy.

I am a human being just like you who believes in family, community service, and kindness to all. It is the callous thinking of society and church leaders that leads many to believe that somehow our lives are devoid of this.

I am grateful for allies who do not stand idly by. I am grateful for allies who not only protest with us in public media forums, but speak out in Sunday School and other spaces where our voices are not heard. I cannot heal on my own.

I will not be erased. I will not be cast aside.

Essays on Relationships

Introduction to Part II

Kerry Spencer Pray

One of the most difficult aspects of discussing queer relationships in the context of Mormonism is the degree to which such discussion is taboo. The LDS Church has been unequivocal in its rejection of queer identities and relationships. But they still occur.

More than that, though, the unspeakableness of our relationships becomes part of the queer Mormon experience. We are connected to people in ways we can't name. What do you name it, when you are in love with a friend, but you don't ever "act" on it? What does it mean to not "act on it"? What of a relationship that spans decades? What about when it ends? Is there a word for that?

I wrote an essay in this section that discusses this with regard to Louise B. Felt and May Anderson. Louise, who was the first General President of the Primary,[1] is thought to have been in a queer relationship with her counselor, May.[2] Louise lived with May and the two shared a home and bed. Louise was technically in a polygamous marriage, but she didn't build her life with her husband, who was largely absent. She built it with her . . . friend?

We can call these two friends if we want. The people of their time called them "ardent lovers,"[3] but we can call them friends if we want to. What gay Mormon woman does not know what it's like to have a "friend"?

Queer people are familiar with having not enough words to describe the complexity of our experiences and having to make them up. Colburn and colleagues argue that women who are closeted within Christian church communities often find themselves having to eschew institutional definitions and to take "authorship of their stories."[4] Ritchie and Barker similarly note that language often has to be invented because current language is simply insufficient.[5]

And sometimes we cannot find the words. Sometimes, the taboo swallows all of them.

One way this manifested in this section is in the difficulty we had getting people to talk to us about their relationships. Polyamorous experiences, in particular, were extraordinarily difficult to get people to talk about openly. Polyamory is something often undertaken in mixed orientation marriages—the regularity with which it is practiced in modern Mormonism would surprise many people. I was surprised, when I entered my first secret queer Mormon spaces on Facebook and found so many people in mixed orientation marriages that were open or polyamorous. The practicality of it, more than anything, is what impressed me. Creating relationships outside the traditional Mormon hetero-nuclear allows the preservation of community while making room for a person's actual propensity to form a certain type of bond. At the minimum, it's sometimes done to simply give the people in the marriage—who were often very young and sexually inexperienced when they entered their marriages—the chance to have concrete experiences upon which to decide whether to attempt to preserve the marriage. It's unreasonable to expect people to leave behind *everything* on the basis of no experience. Such a decision is often made near the end of a mixed orientation marriage, and most such marriages do end,[6] but the experience is still a vital part of negotiating the relationship. I personally know many people in polyamorous relationships, and many people with open marriages.[7] So far, I do not personally know any queer Mormons who have regretted opening their marriages.

And yet, even with the assurance that we would allow the use of pen names and anonymous essays, it was next to impossible to get people to go on the record about them. The taboo is just so strong.

The taboo against polyamory, in particular, is complicated for bisexuals by the heavy biphobia they often experience pertaining to their ability to form monogamous relationships with fidelity. Stereotypes of bisexuals paint them *all* as polyamorous, and paint this as something that is bad. Too many people believe being poly means you are sexually frenzied and incapable of not cheating, when, in actuality, most polyamorous relationships are much more about long-term commitment and emotional support. The reality is, some people are polyamorous. Some are not. This is as much true for bisexuals as anyone else. I know many monogamous bisexuals and many non-bisexuals who are poly. The one essay we have included about polyamory is from someone who is bisexual, but it should not be taken as the *only* form of this type of relationship.

The fundamental challenge of this chapter comes down to this: humans are complex and our language to describe what we mean to each other is so limited. Sometimes, we have only silence. But the space within that silence isn't empty. It's filled with love and with pain and with heartbreak and with a thousand other emotions we cannot name. Because we mean so much to each other.

Our relationships are sacred, whether or not they are recognized. Our relationships are what give our lives meaning, what makes exquisite our pain, what show us how important it is to live our lives with love, and what living our lives with love means.

Many of the essays in this book are written under pen names or are anonymous. In this chapter, there is an added level of utility to this: the anonymity protects not just the author, but also the other people in the essays. Names and identifying details were omitted and changed when necessary to protect not just the authors, but the people they have had relationships with. In an article about honesty and polyamorous relationships, Jingshu Zhu discusses the way "the supposedly ethical practice of truth-telling can turn hurtful,"[8] and harm is something we very much wanted to avoid in telling these delicate stories about relationships that are precious to us.

NOTES

1. "Primary" is the children's organization in the LDS Church. It organizes activities for children from ages three to eleven. Its leadership is local, regional, and global. The General President oversees Primary for the worldwide church. The Primary, along with the Young Women's organization (the LDS Church program for girls ages twelve to seventeen), and the Relief Society (the women's organization), are the only general church programs that are nominally run by women, though these women are still subject to male authority.
2. Michael D. Quinn, *Same-Sex Dynamics Among Nineteenth Century Americans: A Mormon Example* (Urbana: University of Illinois Press, 1996), 231–64.
3. Quinn, *Same-Sex*, 243.
4. K.O. Coburn et al., "The Christian Closet: A Phenomenological Study of Queer Christian Women's Navigation of Church Communities," *Journal of Feminist Family Therapy* 31, no. 4 (2019): 187.
5. A. Ritchie and M. Barker, "'There Aren't Words for What We Do or How We Feel So We Have To Make Them Up': Constructing Polyamorous Languages in a Culture of Compulsory Monogamy," *Sexualities* 9, no. 5 (2006): 584–601.

6. John P. Dehlin et al., "Psychosocial Correlates of Religious Approaches to Same-Sex Attraction: A Mormon Perspective," *Journal of Gay & Lesbian Mental Health* 18, no. 3 (2014): 284–311.

7. Polyamorous relationships take many forms, only one of which is an open relationship. Though typically polyamorous relationships include a sexual aspect, they do not always. Like Ani Ritchie and Meg Barker, I like Anderlini-D'Onofrio's definition: "Polyamory is a form of non-monogamy grounded in the belief in 'people's capacity to share and multiply their love in honest and consensual ways'" (Ritchie and Barker, 584).

8. Zhu Jingshu, "'We're Not Cheaters': Polyamory, Mixed-Orientation Marriage and the Construction of Radical Honesty," *Graduate Journal of Social Science* 14, no. 1 (2018): 59.

I Do Not Sing for My Husband

Jenny Smith

10

Most of my memories are music. My grandfather, sitting at the Tabernacle organ,[1] his fingers dancing across the keys. Duets sung by my parents as I drift to sleep, safely tucked beneath my Holly Hobbie bedspread. A lullaby to my firstborn son as he lay in the clear plastic incubator.

Music has always been part of my life. It thrums through my blood and skates across my skin. I sing in the car. I sing in the shower. I sing at work. I sing through the highs and lows of life, belting my emotions into the void in an effort to reach catharsis no appointment with my therapist will ever bring.

I do not sing for my husband.

My best friend tells me this is odd; she sings to her husband all the time. "It's what musical people do," she says. I am a musical person therefore it follows I should sing to the people I love.

I sing for my children. I sing for my ward. I sing for my coworkers. I once sang for a group of drunken Jews at a karaoke bar following an Orthodox wedding.

I do not sing for my husband.

I Spoke to You with Silence

Anonymous

11

I called to you once from inside a closet. (The metaphor, I know. It's almost too much. But it happened.) I had just emptied it out and was looking at the back wall as if it was the first time, though it must not have been. The paint on the inside was peeling. Decades of mixed colors—green, grey, white. The carpet on the floor of the closet was at least fifty years old.

"Come look," I said. "There's a door here. In the back of the closet, there's a door." This ancient house had always been full of surprises.

You came to me and stood close enough I could smell the soap you used. You wore a gold chain around your neck and it was as if the smell came from there, though I remember thinking it must actually be your hair, which you always kept short, and always smelled of soap. "Where did it go?" you asked. "To the outside somewhere? How old is this door?"

"Old," I said. "There's a porch there now. It's starting to fall down, it's so old. But this must have been a way out. You used to be able to walk outside from here."

"Where does it lead now?"

"To a crawlspace, if anywhere. I don't know. Somewhere dark. Somewhere we couldn't go, even if we wanted to go there."

On a Tuesday, you were making a pie crust.

Flour dusted the tops of the counters of your kitchen, and I held it between my fingers, feeling the gritty friction.

A baby was in a bouncy chair in the doorway. *Bounce, bounce, bounce, bounce,* he went, and on each bounce, he made a sound. *Ah, ah, ah, ah.*

You laughed at him.

"Do you ever wish you could remember what it felt like?" I asked. "To bounce up and down and up and down? To have no thought of loneliness, no thought of hunger or despair? Just the feeling of the floor beneath your feet?"

"Oh, he is going to be hungry in approximately five minutes." You rolled the dough into a perfectly round, perfectly thin layer. You folded it over, dusted it with flour, and you rolled it again.

"I don't know how you do that," I said. "How you get it to be so perfectly round."

"It is a gift I have," you said. "One of my more important ones."

Once, I let you touch me.

We had been outside, wading through the waist-high grass of my back field, on our way to where I'd planted the squash and the cucumbers. The babies were playing on the swings, far from us, and we could hear them: the creak of the ropes, the shuffle of the bark beneath their feet, laughter.

I bent over to pick a gourd that had grown wild and my back spasmed hard and I couldn't stand up. You walked behind me as I hobbled back to the house, watched as I angled myself down onto the floor.

"Let me see if I can help," you said. "I'm good with this sort of thing."

I shook my head. *No, no. We don't touch,* I thought. *That is the rule of this relationship. That is the thing that can never, ever change.* "It's not that bad," I said. (It was a lie.)

You didn't listen to me, and you put the knuckle of your hand against my bare skin. You pushed against the muscle. The carpet underneath my face felt like acrylic. I could smell the polymer they used to glue it down.

I started to cry. I let you think it was because it hurt. I may have even said it was because it hurt. But that's not why I was crying.

On a Thursday you came to my house. I was sitting on the floor, my back to the couch, watching the baby throw toys around the room.

"I'm so tired," I told you. "My body feels so tired. There has to be more than this. I give him everything I have until I am empty and there is nothing left and nowhere to fill me back up."

The baby put a rubbery animal that looked like a cross between a lion and a giraffe into his mouth. I watched the stream of drool that dripped down his chin, watched it fly across the room and onto the floor as he shook the toy.

You picked the baby up and he grabbed your face between his hands. The giraffe was tossed aside as you exclaimed, "Kisses!" and he immediately put your entire chin into his mouth.

His drool dripped down the side of your face and you squeezed your eyes shut. "Kisses!" you said again, though it was more like a scream as you endured the onslaught of his affection. He tilted his head and looked you in the eyes, adoration plain.

I wondered how it must feel—to take your cheeks between hands, to put a mouth on your face, to feel so little shame over any of it.

Once we drove in the middle of the night. I don't remember why. There weren't babies with us (there were usually babies with us—for so many years, there were babies with us). We drove up to the top of the mountain. It was too windy to get all the way out, but we opened our doors and stood up so we could see down below.

"Does it look different up here?" I asked.

The air was cold, but not frozen. I could smell mud, so there must have been rain.

You were wearing a high-necked T-shirt and mom jeans.

"Sometimes I want to leave my husband," you said to me.

"Why don't you?"

You laughed.

"Really. Why don't you?"

"Because," you said, "it would be unkind."

"When was the last time you were happy?" There were cars driving through the canyons down below and I watched them.

You didn't look at me. You looked like you were looking where I was looking. Down, down, far away. "I'm happy when I'm with you."

"It's good to be kind," I said. "But you have to be kind to yourself, too."

You held onto the car door for a long time before you got back in. I watched the way the folds of your knuckles curved against the gold of your wedding band. "I remember what you were wearing," you said, "on that day when I first met you. I remember the way the collar folded against your neck."

"That was so long ago," I said. "We were so young then."

The wind blew and your hair blew with it. It brushed against your glasses. Your tennis shoe made a squeaking sound where it rested on the floor-end of the open car door. "Has it all been a waste?" you asked me. "All of these years. And we have never—" You didn't finish the sentence.

I wanted to say it couldn't be. But it felt like a lie.

I saw your hand shake as you took a breath. You looked at me and you looked away. I can still hear the sound your jeans made as the fabric ran across the passenger's seat when you sat down.

The steering wheel felt cold against my hands and I wanted to say something—anything.

We had never, not even once, crossed the line.

But we didn't need to touch to have been bonded.

That was the greatest lie of it all.

That this was only a sin if we touched.

That this was only *real* if we touched.

That this . . . it can't be gay if you never, ever touch.

But I loved you.

I loved you.

"Do you remember that night, I think it was just before your nineteenth birthday?"

The chair I was sitting on was hard, but it was quiet outside. (I liked the quiet.) I could hear the wind, blowing through the grass, could hear birds, but they were somewhere far off, far in the distance.

"We were driving and that song came on by Queen. *You're my best friend.* You sang it so loud. And I sang it back. And we sang and we drove."

I shook my head. "I don't," I said. "I don't remember."

"It felt so important. The singing. The words. All of it."

I went still. Still enough I could hear the hum of cars, driving on a distant road. "How many decades ago was that?" I asked.

"Too many," you said.

Once, I told you I loved you.

Not as a friend.

It was late at night. I had a baby asleep on my chest. I was getting too old to have babies asleep on my chest. Too old for secrets that were too hard to keep. "For so many years," I said, "I've loved you."

You didn't say anything at first.

I had the thought that I had broken something. That I *knew* I had broken something.

I thought I could hear in your silence an admonition. *This is the thing we don't speak. This is the thing we are not allowed to speak.*

"Of course, I loved you, too," you said. "Of course, I did. Of course, I do. But I . . . I'm not . . . We can't."

Some doors you can't walk through, you can't walk out, there is only darkness.

If I said anything back, I didn't want to.

The last time I saw you I think I knew I wouldn't see you again. You were getting out of the car, and I reached out. "Stop," I said. And I reached for your hand.

You took it.

You had a bag slung over a shoulder. It fell down to your elbow as you pulled me to you, and you hugged me.

For decades, there was no one but you. For decades, I'd loved no one the way I loved you. It wasn't supposed to be a final goodbye, but I think, somehow, I knew it would be.

I cried as I left. I didn't say your name out loud. I wouldn't have. I spoke to you with silence, the way I had always spoken the truest things to you.

I don't know if you ever heard.

On the Side of Love

Bobbie Lee-Corry

12

It was a hot June morning, and we were speed walking. In what I can only explain as an impossible dream come true, my LDS Chinese parents trailed after my spouse and me, the first time they had visited the USA during Pride month.

"Let's hurry!" called my wife as she ran ahead. "It's going to start soon!"

My parents and I picked up our pace, and before she cut in front of me, I quickly caught my mom's hand.

"Mom," I started, "it means so much that you and Dad are here with us."

My mom nodded, pulling me along to keep step with my spouse and dad.

"Truly, Mom," I said. "I never imagined we'd get here like this. Thank you."

She smiled. "Of course," she said. "We're happy to be here. Now, come on, they're starting!"

Nothing could have prepared me for the rush of gratitude and love I felt for her and my father in that moment.

My parents were walking in the pride parade with us, actively choosing to show their love and support of their child and new daughter-in-law.

I tried so hard not to ugly-cry, but the truth is, like many others, most of my life had been filled with deep shame and emotional isolation. And this wasn't because I let my attractions define me—because I didn't—but my religion did. I was taught that, even after everything I could do right in this life, I would still be unworthy to enter into the highest kingdom of Heaven if I wasn't married to a man; I couldn't be with God if I wasn't married to a man. And I definitely could not be with my family forever if I was married to, well, anyone who wasn't a man.

That took a toll on me—a child who wanted to grow up to love and be loved. A child who was horrified to learn that their desire to have a family with someone they love is akin to deviant behavior like lying, cheating, promiscuity, and killing.

I came out five years ago and to this day, I am still the only out gay person in the Singapore Stake. Yes, we have just one LDS stake in Singapore. I know there are other kids like me, but no one else has come out. I don't blame them. After a while, you can't decide who you'd disappoint more, your Mormon elders or your Chinese elders or, in my case, probably both.

So in the meantime, it has been a very, very lonely space to be in. But I am grateful to be out because I can now be someone I wish I had when I was younger. I hope that I can be someone that an LGBTQ person in the Singapore Stake knows they can reach out to, especially knowing that many parents in the stake talk amongst themselves about my being gay. Sometimes, I wish they'd just talk *to* me. One time a sweet mother in the stake did. She came to me and said, "I just want you to know I love you for who you are and that you deserve to be happy. I'm here for you." And only then did I know this mother was a safe person I could talk to.

For a long time, my parents felt they were the only ones, especially my mother. I want you to know that my parents not only love and support me, but they now love and support me openly. It hasn't always been this way. Being open and proud of me is a very difficult thing. What would their friends and our extended family think? So no, it hasn't been easy; it rarely is. And no, not everything is "perfect" and dandy now. They still struggle with using my correct pronouns, and sometimes they don't know how to ask the right questions, but I know they are trying their best, and that is more than I can ask for.

A little while ago, my partner's dad asked my father, "So how did you come to the conclusion to love and support your daughter?" My father replied, "Given my beliefs, I could err on either side, but I realized that if I erred on the side of not loving my child, there would easily be a lot worse outcomes, so I knew that I'd rather err on the side of love."

13

Cute
A Polycule
Bea Goodman

"What level of lesbian is 'building a grill'?" asks my girlfriend's husband.

"We're bisexuals," I correct him with a laugh, circling the box on the kitchen floor. I reach in to loosen the top piece, but I can't even get anything to even jiggle.

Lee is out running DoorDash, and we're assembling the gift Dave got her for their two-year wedding anniversary.

He flips through the instruction booklet, and the corrugated cardboard hisses as I cut through it. Dave spins around and sighs with relief.

"I'm just cutting it down to access everything inside."

"You're good. I know the gas line isn't connected to anything, but I had to check."

I haul back on the now-isolated sides of the box, laying it flat so we can access its contents. I start pulling away packaging: the cardboard dry, the plastic smooth and cool. It doesn't take long before the entire room is scattered with metal pieces in their protective boxes and bags.

"Is there an instruction book or something?" I ask Dave.

"Yeah, here you go."

I flip through the glossy pages to the first few steps. I skip the free app download and start looking for the base and legs of the grill. I also find the five little baggies of screws and gadgets to hold this thing together. I don't see the scissors nearby, so I stand and pick my way through the debris to get them from the front room.

Dave is now looking through the booklet and pulling packing material from actual grill parts. After only a few minutes, it's easier to hand him the tools to attach pieces from his side while I work from mine.

We flow from one step to the next. Most of our conversation consists of "Where's the screwdriver now?" or "Okay, pass me the next screw."

It takes us three tries to get the gas line and the electrical wires all threaded correctly under the main cooking element.

"Okay, now that we've detached it again, I can lift it and you can pull it out," I direct, having already lifted the unit twice.

"Yeah, I'm good at pulling things out," he manages to say this with a straight face while I sigh in relief.

"Thank you! I've been thinking about so many of those jokes this entire time but holding them in!" I pick up the hollow shell for the actual grilling while he redirects the flexible elements through the appropriate channels.

After, Dave starts, "If Lee was here—"

I cut him off. "—there would be a lot more 'that's what she said' jokes, I know!"

He cocks his head before adding, "I was going to say there would be a lot more F-words, but that's also true."

I return the nod while I pop open my water bottle. We've hit a few bumpy sections of assembling this grill, but we make a good team. The entire thing is finished after an hour and a half of serious finagling, and Dave messages Lee in our group chat: "Lee, you have a grill."

She responds with a smiley face.

"Bea helped a ton," Dave adds. "Like seriously."

"She's cute, I guess" is what Lee says, and I just laugh.

A few hours later, we are sitting in a row: me, Lee, and Dave. All three of us fit on the futon when we want to. I lean against pillows on my end, Dave against a pile of blankets on the other, and Lee brushes arms with both of us. Lee's unfinished burger is sitting on the ottoman in front of us. The air smells of grass and summer sun wafting in through the open window on the other side of the small room.

Dave finds a meme on Reddit that makes him exhale and he turns the phone screen to show us each in turn.

"Send that to me," Lee says with a chuckle.

"Put it in the group," I add.

A moment later, my phone buzzes in my hand. Dave's picture has come through. I swipe it away, knowing it's safe. I glance at Lee and can't help but say, "You're cute." I kiss her arm, the closest bit of her I can reach.

She scrunches her face, reluctant to accept the compliment.
"Yeah, you are," Dave adds from her other side, and she grins.
We each breathe in our own rhythm, creating a symphony of three.
I am safe.

Wedding Dress

14

Anonymous

September 2019

"How would you feel if I wore a jumpsuit?"

My fiancé and I were curled up in his basement room, watching a Minecraft video. I'd come out to him as nonbinary almost a year earlier. He didn't mind. He just loved me for who I was.

"What?" he said. Then, connecting the dots, he added, "I thought you had a dress."

"I do. But I'm not sure if I hate it."

His brows furrowed over his eyes. "Why would you hate it?"

I turned away from him, closed my eyes. "I don't know. It doesn't feel like *me*. Something about it isn't right."

And yet, I knew, it was right that shining golden day I put it on for the first time. What does it mean to start crying when you put on The Dress? Isn't that the sign that it is, in fact, The Dress?

"I'd like it if you wore a dress. I always imagined the person I married wearing a dress."

"Oh," I said. "Okay."

But I still snuck back to the website to eye the jumpsuit again and again and again.

December 2019

There were four weeks until the wedding, and only two until finals week, on the day of my bridal shower. My mother and sisters were on their way to Lincoln from Omaha. And me? I wasn't wearing pants to my wedding, but I was going to wear them to my party. My lilac pantsuit was every bit as perfect as it was when I bought it nine months earlier in Rome. I paired it with a navy blue and white striped sweater to match my blue suede heels. The trouser leg draped onto the heel of the shoe. I looked dignified. Refined. Elegant. Like me.

"I didn't realize we were supposed to dress up," my seventeen-year-old sister said as I slid into the car. She wore a slouchy sweatshirt and jeans.

"You weren't," I said. "I'm the bride, so I can be as fancy as I want."

And that day, I wanted pants.

Like that jumpsuit. The halter neck plunged downwards into a V, stopping below the breastbone. A thin belt separated the top from the wide-legged pants. The crisp lines would frame my waist, my hips, my legs. The ivory color wouldn't wash me out in photographs. It even had pockets.

I'd returned to the website over and over for seven months to ogle the jumpsuit, but hadn't bought it. I wanted it. More than I'd ever wanted a piece of clothing before. Yet I wouldn't—couldn't—make that purchase. Not when I could picture the betrayed disappointment in my fiancé's eyes.

January 2020

My wedding day dawned cold and clear. No snow. No ice. Just temperatures hovering around freezing.

I wore a dress.

Love and Change

15

Blaire Ostler

It was early Sunday morning when Drew gently called from the bathroom, "Good morning, beautiful. It's time to get up. We can't be late for church." He was already awake, showered, and dressed before I even opened my eyes.

Still lying in bed, I opened my eyes and replied, "Or you could come back to bed and we could have our own spiritual experience."

He paused ever so briefly, weighing his options before abruptly blurting out, "With God as my witness, we are going to be on time to church! Get your beautiful ass out of bed and get dressed."

We exchanged smiles as I begrudgingly got out of bed. Drew walked over to the closet and pulled out a necktie. "I think I'll wear my purple tie with my rainbow button to church today. That way I can support the ordination of women and the LGBTQ community."

Sometimes I have to pinch myself after he says things like that. If you would have told me ten years ago my husband would be supporting the ordination of women and the queer community, I wouldn't have believed you. Not my husband.

As I watched him pin his button onto his jacket, my mind recalled an unpleasant memory.

It was 2008. Prop 8 was all over the news.[1] Drew and I had been arguing for years about homosexuality. We didn't need to be reminded of our blatant disagreement every time the news came on, but there it was. Again.

Drew commented while staring at the screen, "They want to get married now. Soon they'll want to be teaching it in schools."

I routinely said, "There's nothing wrong with being gay."

He countered, "Did you read Elder Oaks's conference talk on homosexuality I sent you?"

I flatly replied, "Yes."

He continued, "Blaire, the prophet has spoken about this. You need to get a testimony for yourself. Being gay is wrong."

I replied, "The prophet is wrong. They aren't much different from me."

Drew scoffed, "You're nothing like them. You may be attracted to women, but you're not one of them."

I interjected, "I'm everything like them! How can you separate them from me? How can you accept me and not them?"

He responded, "Jeez, why are you so upset? You're overreacting."

I couldn't continue. We had fought too many fights. I couldn't handle another. "Drew, I don't want to fight anymore. I have read all the books and conference talks you have asked me to read. We've said all that can be said, and neither one of us has changed."

He continued, "But Blaire—"

I cut him off, "Drop it! I can't even look at your face!" I exhaled, trying to regain my composure. I continued softly and brokenly, "I really don't want to fight anymore. It hurts too much."

Seeing my frustration, he gently put his hand on my shoulder and said, "Okay. I'll drop it."

Not another word was spoken. We both knew our marriage wouldn't survive it.

Years went by with little conversation about homosexuality. It came up here and there. We casually discussed it from time to time, but we stopped aggressively trying to convert each other. Forcibly trying to change the other person only led to more heartache. Instead, we focused on loving each other.

Somewhere along the way, something changed. I don't know exactly why or how it happened. You'd have to ask Drew for the details, which I'm sure are many. But slowly over the years, something gradually changed.

More time passed. It was an average day of housework until my phone rang. I picked up. "Hey, honey. How's work going? I was just thinking about you."

Drew spoke slowly and quietly, "Blaire, do you realize you're bisexual?"

I awkwardly agreed. "Yes. I know I'm bisexual."

He continued, "Yes, but *you* are bisexual."

It was as if every conversation we had over the last decade merged into a single moment of clarity for him. He realized there are orientations beyond gay or straight, and bisexuality wasn't simply a myth. Growing up in the church, he never considered the possibility that he would fall in love with a bisexual woman, when queer women were distant, othered, and inherently broken.

I laughed. I didn't know how to respond to his realization. I had been bisexual our entire marriage and tried my best to make that clear to him, but hearing him accept the label somehow made it real.

Smiling, I said the only thing I could say, "I know I'm bisexual. What took you so long?"

Drew answered with such sincerity, "I couldn't ... I didn't ... I'm sorry. You're a beautiful, wonderful, bisexual woman, and there's nothing wrong with you. I love you."

I smiled and replied, "I've waited a long time to hear you say that."

He continued with remorse in his tone, "Why did you stay married to me? All the things I've said to you. After all these years, why?"

I paused, holding back the tears. "Loving you seemed more important than agreeing with you."

The memories faded as I stood next to Drew watching him put on his purple tie for church. I didn't need to pinch myself. The moment was real. I commented, "It's still weird to hear you say things like that."

He replied, "Say things like what?"

I continued, "Your support for the queer community. I didn't think I would ever hear these things from you, but here you are with your purple tie and rainbow button."

He smiled. "Thanks for waiting for me."

Hearts change. People change. Beliefs change. Change is sometimes subtle, laborious, or slow, but part of enabling change means loving people enough to let it happen on their terms. Sometimes you love them enough to stay. Sometimes you love them enough to let them go. Sometimes you love them enough to listen instead of speak. Sometimes you love them enough to put their desires before your own. Sometimes you love them so much it hurts. Your love doesn't guarantee the people you love will change in the ways you want them to, but I do believe love is the only way forward.

NOTE

1. Proposition 8 was a measure on the California ballot in 2008. It proposed a state constitutional amendment to outlaw same-sex marriages. The Mormon Church was extremely active in promoting Proposition 8, and their labor and financial contributions are thought to have contributed to the measure passing. It was eventually ruled unconstitutional on the federal level.

Noticed
Anonymous

16

"So, what have you been up to since you got back from your mission?"

We stand in an overcrowded line, surrounded by well-dressed people and small talk.

She and I go through all the classic, mundane get-to-know-you questions. I tell her I'm back in school, she tells me she's back home with her family for the summer but that she's coming back to Provo in the fall.

The venue is a nice, open space with red brick, soft yellow string lights, and green and white flower arrangements laid out meticulously on long, dark wooden tables—the perfect location for a wedding reception.

The bride is a mutual friend of ours; her trainee, my old roommate. She and I only spoke once or twice in the mission field and, honestly, I couldn't even begin to try and remember what it was about. But, seeing as she and I are both having a shortage of acquaintances in the sea of childhood friends and family of the bride and groom, we grab a hold of what few common ties we have and stick together.

It's late summer in Las Vegas, so the air outside feels stale and hot and the air inside feels cool and artificial. I don't wear dresses often, but I'm sporting the nicest one I have—black, with a lace pattern and half-length sleeves that are just a little too flowy for my taste. Her dress is baby blue with thin, white stripes running down it. She borrowed it from a friend, so she's anxious about keeping it in good shape.

"Did you drive or fly down?" I ask.

"I drove down with my parents. They're actually right over there—you should sit with us!" She motions for her mom to save an extra seat at their table.

We talk about road trips, about the west coast and forests and beaches and going on adventures and all of a sudden, the moment of polite awkwardness is past, and I feel like I'm talking with an old friend. We sit down to eat and she introduces me to her parents. All three of them are of such a similar disposition: quiet, reserved, but the kindest, warmest, friendliest, most genuine type of people—the kind of people who make you feel like you matter by the way they talk and listen to you.

"Mom, she served Spanish-speaking!" She had told me earlier that her mother's first language is Spanish and that she had wished more than anything that she could have had the same language assignment on her mission as I'd had.

Her mother has dark brown eyes. Her entire being—her smile, her expressions, her body language—all personify gentleness and warmth. She and her husband tell the two of us that we need to try the churros out back. I finish my dinner and we go out together.

As I'm eating, talking, smiling, laughing, I begin to notice her more. Her eyes are a lighter, almost greenish brown; her hair is brown with soft, golden highlights; her smile radiates warmth—she's just so genuine and fun and beautiful and—

Oh shit.

My heart jumps, then it drops, then it begins to race, and I wonder if she noticed.

I try to ignore it, try to be calm and casual and act like I had been acting all night but now it feels forced. The DJ calls for the father-daughter dance, then the bouquet toss, then opens the floor to the guests. She goes off with a family she and the bride had taught as missionaries and I go off with my ride, but I can't help looking over at her, thinking about her, wanting to be next to her again.

We send the bride and groom off and my ride and I grab our things and get ready to leave. I hug her goodbye, say it was good to see her, she says she'll see me at school, and I turn around and head for the exit. Her mother sees me going and stops me to say goodbye.

"It was *so great* to meet you. I hope we see you when we drive down to Provo in the fall!" She hugs me tight and smiles at me.

I smile back. "It was great to meet you, too. Drive home safe!"

The air outside is dry and warm, even though the sun went down hours ago. It's dark and a few faint stars stand out against the lights of the city.

I change out of my dress and into my sweats and settle into the backseat of the car for the drive home. I try to sleep, but the same thought keeps running through my mind: I've never fallen for someone that fast.

About a month later I show up late to a game night with some friends (an old roommate from the mission had invited me). When I walk in, I see her. It had been long enough that I'd convinced myself that what I had felt for her that night at the reception was nothing—a minor crush at best.

I sit down across the room and make casual, awkward conversation with the stranger next to me: "So where are you from?"

I glance at her and notice that she's looking at me. My heart jumps and drops and races all over again in the brief moment that our eyes meet. I wonder if she noticed, if she could notice, me. And I realize this isn't just a minor crush.

Months have passed by, but I still think about her. Even though I know it could never happen and that I should just get over it and move on, I can't help it.

And I still wonder if she ever noticed.

Ordinary Magnificent

Kerry Spencer Pray

17

Sometimes, when I look at Heather, I remember another life.

They are fleeting memories, strange in their specificity.

She will be standing in front of the stove, baseball cap on backwards as she swings a kitchen rag over her shoulder and stirs. She'll turn her hips just slightly as she rocks her weight from one foot to the other, lifting up the wooden spoon to taste the sauce. And then, without warning, it's like I see her, superimposed, on another Heather, from another time. I'll see a different style of clothing, a different sweep of hair. Sometimes I see her as a woman. Sometimes I don't.

Mormons don't really believe in reincarnation—not this kind. They don't believe that we come back to earth again and again, in one life after another. And even though I adore all of the many aspects of what my friend Mette calls "woo-woo spirituality," I have never been one to necessarily believe (or not believe) in any of them. Who can say what to make of a fleeting vision. Our minds are strange caverns of will, memory, and biochemistry.

Some people think the first General Primary President, Louise Felt, was in a same-sex relationship with her counselor, May Anderson. They lived together, worked together, were called the most "ardent lovers,"[1] and sometimes they stayed up late at night, in their bathrobes, working and talking next to each other in bed.[2] Louise did not live with her polygamous husband, as far as we know. She built her life with May.

Skeptics say their love was platonic, that there was no reason to assume it was sexual.

Skeptics are always quick to fall back to the idea of sex, of body parts, as if their presence or absence is the sum total of what it means to be queer.

I spoke this week with my friend Rachel about my experience with queerness. She was working on a book of poetry about Heavenly Mother and wanted to include some poems that spoke to the queer Mormon experience.

We spoke at length; we did not speak of either sex or body parts.

The other night, Heather was watching a reality TV show. Celebrities wore various costumes—monsters, ravens, aliens, pineapples. Their faces were obscured and a panel tried to guess who they were based on their voices alone.

I lay next to her, playing Candy Crush until I ran out of lives—then I'd reset the clock on my phone to get more lives.

Her foot was underneath the covers, the sole of it resting against my leg. My skin was cold and her skin was warm.

All day long, the Utah State legislature had been debating a bill on conversion therapy. The public comment period was filled with stories of people who'd been "cured," their wicked inclinations purged, their heterosexual-passing marriages now pure, due to a practice that has more in common with torture than therapy—a practice that has been shown to increase suicides, and be utterly unsuccessful in changing orientation.[3]

"*This*," I said to her, leaning my head against her arm. "This is the thing they want to change. The thing they find so unnatural. The fact that I want to lie next to you in bed, our skin touching. I want to cheat at Candy Crush while you watch terrible television and that is so horrible it is worth torturing children, sometimes literally to death."

She looked at me and she didn't say anything.

It took me a long time to admit that I wasn't straight. That there was something different about the way I tended to form bonds, about the people I tended to form them with. I had been so thoroughly convinced there was something dirty and shameful about being queer. But nothing I'd experienced could remotely be called dirty or shameful, and so I must not be queer.

I would listen to queer people say, "this is about love, this is about identity," and I would be confused. Because it was about sex, about body parts. It was about right and wrong and choices.

Wasn't it?

I have a sense memory, from one of those strange maybe-other lives. We stand in a doorway, looking out. The air is dusty and cold. I can hear horses. We are watching someone go. I don't know who. But I remember the feel of her hip, warm against mine. I remember the too-tight apron ties, pinching my middle. I feel the rustle of fabric as she reaches out and takes my hand. I don't know the context. Maybe the context doesn't matter. Because *she* is the sense. *She* is the memory.

Everyone's experience with queerness is different. But mine ... mine is about love. No matter that I used to hear people say the same thing and say, "yes, but," and not understand. There is not another way to say it.

It is the experience of sitting next to a person I love, in front of a bonfire, a bent coat hanger dangling a hot dog perilously close to the ashes. It is laughing in the passenger seat of a car, weaving in and out of trees and hills, the dark road glistening with salt. It is the heavy relief of my head resting on her shoulder as I read a book. It is dancing in the kitchen, one hand holding a chicken-salad sandwich, the other hand holding hers as I spin around. It is walking next to her at the grocery store. She holds two packages of meat, examining them as if they are remarkably different.

"I'm going to get both," she says, not looking at me.

"We don't need both." I stand behind the cart, because pushing the cart is what I do, and putting things in the cart is what she does.

"We can freeze what we don't need," she says. "Food is important, Kerry."

It is ordinary. Magnificent. But ordinary.

One of the strange aspects of being a queer Mormon comes in reconciling the disconnect between the church's utter rejection of your nontraditional relationships and identities and the fact that Mormon ontology is fundamentally inseparable from nontraditional relationships and identities. These "peculiar people" who travelled across the plains with oxen and handcarts to practice polygamy, who thought nothing of sister wives who formed pair bonds in the sacred absence of husbands, these are the same ones who tell us that a queer marriage is somehow worse than attempted murder.[4] That our love is apostasy.[5]

Sometimes I forget I'm an apostate.

I have a family I love. My relationships bring me joy.

How is that apostasy?

I have only one maybe-other-life memory that involves sex, and it wasn't queer sex. Like all of my other strange memories that my brain may or may not be inventing, it is more sense than memory. I remember the light, coming through slats of wood. I remember the feel of holding something like a shovel, bending over it to scoop feed into a trough. She was my husband then, skinny, not particularly tall. He (*she*) came up behind me and kissed me on the back of my neck. I remember recognizing his (*her*) smell. I remember the sound of my own laugh as I reached behind me, and pulled him (*her*) to me.

In the *now*, my twenty-first-century life, I used to be married to a man. Sex was not a big part of my marriage to him (both of us were gay), and yet no one questioned the legitimacy of that marriage. He was a man, and I was a woman, so no one really cared what we did or did not do behind doors they did not have to walk through.

In the maybe-life, where I laughed in the barn, no one questioned the legitimacy of my marriage, either.

Woo-woo spirituality aside: What does it mean to be queer?

Gender, identity, homosexuality, they may seem strange, as I said when I struggled to explain them to Rachel—to explain what it means to have a nonbinary, female-identifying partner; what it means to have a relationship that is outside of traditional. But our identities and relationships, as different as they seem, aren't aberrant. We are as we were created and this is meaningful. Our inability to convey the strange, mythic beauty of our human variety doesn't diminish it.

"You're wearing my rainbow socks," Heather said to me last night, as she was tangling her feet with mine underneath the covers.

"Honey," I said. "Think of them as *our* rainbow socks."

She shook her head at me. She laughed. Her being a man or being a woman didn't matter at that moment. She pulled me against her and I fell asleep with her arm draped over my hip.

That is what it means.

In this life, in other lives, throughout history. That is all it has ever meant.

NOTES

1. D. Michael Quinn, *Same-Sex Dynamics Among Nineteenth Century Americans: A Mormon Example* (Urbana: University of Illinois Press, 2001), 243.
2. Quinn, *Same-Sex*, 244.
3. C. Ryan, R.B. Toomey and S.T. Russell, "Parent-Initiated Sexual Orientation Change Efforts with LGBT Adolescents: Implications for Young Adult Mental Health and Adjustment," *The Journal of Homosexuality* 7 (November 2018): 1–15.
4. Billy Hallowell, "Mormon Church Just Codified Two Major Policies Involving People 'In Same-Gender Marriage' and Their Children," *The Blaze*, November 6, 2015, https://www.theblaze.com/news/2015/11/06/mormon -church-just-codified-two-major-policies-involving-people-in-same-gender -marriage-and-their-children.

5. This essay was written after the 2015 Mormon handbook decision to classify those in same-sex marriages as "apostates" but before the 2019 decision that reversed those changes. Spouses in a same-sex marriage are now considered "serious sinners" and not "apostates."

18

Melaleuca
Kel Purcill

Of the shaggy Australian melaleuca tree, some three-hundred odd varieties of them, many shed long curls of bark year-round, the tougher outer layer falling back and taking swathes of the fine, deeper sheets with it. Commonly called paperbarks, their bark is nothing like any paper you'd easily find. The inner bark layers are silken, lush, even around the little bumps and divots the supporting trunk or insect boreholes have added. Peel back arboreal time-authored pages and messages left by bugs, fires, and life are revealed across the soft layers, stretch marks of growth and survival. An adult paperbark tree looks relaxed to me, like a fortysomething-year-old woman who's taken off her bra, put her feet up, breathed out long and sweet.

A few years ago, I'm cooking dinner and feeling nostalgic. I haven't seen paperbark in ages but found a random piece on the footpath after work. The whisper-thin edges remind me of being decades younger, hoarding paperbark and writing tiny books in the peeled pages. Of being older, and having so much written against my skin, desire curling long and loose—

"Hey, Mum, do you think God hates queer people?"

My eldest, Patrick, barely adult, leans against the counter to poke the paperbark.

"Nope," I said, pushing the beauty closer to him. "Not a chance."

"So you don't think queer people are automatically outcast? Or going to outer darkness?"

"No way." This is instant, utter, absolute. *Do I tell him? About me?*

He fiddles around for a minute, starts slowly teasing a piece of paperbark back.

"Why don't you think that? Don't they say being gay is a sin or something?" he asks, easing the layers apart.

"Honey, there's a difference between what the church thinks and what God thinks. I believe, think, *know* the church is wrong. Love is love is love."

Patrick has successfully freed a sheet of fine, translucent paperbark the size of his palm, runs it carefully between his fingertips.

"Sweetie," I tell him, stripping tougher outer bark into wispy tendrils, "don't ever let someone tell you who you can and can't love. Whoever tells you that is a jerk. That's what I think."

"Yeah, me, too. Thanks, Ma." He leans down, gently knocks shoulders with me and heads off up the hallway.

The paperbark on the counter is soft. It reminds me of people and places I've kissed and loved. Maybe I should start dating again.

Years later, my youngest told me they were trans on the fifth day of Patrick's suicide watch.

I knew the announcement was coming. My youngest has always lived with their heart in high-definition, eleventy-billion decibel, fifty meters in every direction subtlety. The signs were there:

"Geez, the news sucks today. Why, Mum, why do homophobes think that behavior's okay?" and,

"Pronouns are important. And it's not like they're hard. Can I help with dinner?"

And a thousand other comments, conversations, brushstrokes, and melodies that made up my youngest, second child. *Should I tell them? That I'm not straight? Would that help?*

I decided it wouldn't.

It was a song I would not sing.

I knew an announcement was coming, just like their seventeenth birthday. The nouns didn't matter to me—my kids knowing I loved them did. Loving my kids meant realizing the church was damaging them, hurting all of us, so we stepped away.

We stepped away, and I saw myself again. How as a convert to the church, chunks of myself were hacked away. Then whittled. Then pared back one translucent, stuttering hangnail at a time. Throughout it all, there was a song I could not sing.

We stepped away, watched bruises fade, but I woke constantly rubbing my knuckles. I dreamed of my hated childhood enemy: a cranky, splinter-spitting tree in the park opposite my house. Every dream was spent falling down the trunk, losing skin and patience and chunks of knuckle. I'd launch awake, flexing my hands, the dream still sap-thick and stubborn against my skin. Always the same dream, always the same chunks of knuckle.

I fell down the trunk again. *I'm not straight,* I told the tree while sucking on a sour, bloody divot on my hand. *I haven't said that in years.*

Another scrape down the trunk. *I'm not straight, and I don't have to pretend because of church.*

The next plummet chewed my cheek and an elbow as well. *I have no clue how to tell my kids or friends.* I was still falling.

I want to climb a different tree, I groused in my dream.

Then woke, laughing.

Paperbarks' nectar feed a huge range of native birds, insects, and endangered flying foxes, and the trees themselves often are part of a complicated ecosystem of other flora, insect lifecycles, and fauna. The paperbark tree's loose, almost spongy outer bark has a high water content, the secret folds and resources protecting the inner trunk in times of bushfire, drought, and winds.

Loving my kids and the changes life had delivered to them meant over the past few months I had researched gender fluidity, epilepsy medications, chronic illnesses, and safe sex practices. I finished my degree, at the excellent age of fortysomething. I daydreamed of dating again, hope and wariness wrestling constantly. I investigated depression statistics in chronic illness studies, the appalling self-harm and suicide rates of queer teens and young adults. I downloaded a dating app, post- and LDS-adjacent studies and essays, learned about upcoming book and movie releases, throat singing, and new Yorkshire pudding recipes. These were my kids, and I would protect, encourage, and help them every and any way I could.

I knew the announcement was coming. The suicide watch was a complete tit-punch. Not serious enough to be hospitalized, too dire to be left alone, Patrick joined my youngest and I in our little apartment days two weeks before Christmas. Cicadas screamed outside in the Australian summer heat while my nerves shrieked at how to keep my adult child alive, here, *alive, dammit.*

All three of us sweated. The aircon worked perfectly, a baseline thrum to the days and nights where none of us could settle, while we steeped in our own stews of futures unmet. Our skins sat wrong that week: my youngest finding every clothing seam too harsh and every corner of furniture hungry for their bones, my twenty-year-old sagging, curling impossibly small within his favorite blanket, grim lines chewing into his face. The skin too tight around my shoulders, terror sweating along unfamiliar paths on my back as I looked at my children, as I went over my research.

Somewhere in the mess I deleted the dating app from my phone.

I hoped. Worried. Mourned. Loved. Swore. Fretted.

Loved wildly, hugely, with every frantic atom of my entire self. The universe collapsed then magnified to three bodies spinning in space, close enough to touch, a whisper from disaster, overlapping orbits and breathless and beautiful and bewildering.

I hated the pong of my telltale armpits, breathed into my bones the weary green of my eldest's sadness when I checked on him every hour through the night. He smelt of grasses going brown in drought, the sea-thickened sigh of the drowning, the dust not even halfway through a rough, crushing journey.

I swore at the tension concreting my shoulders, watched the grace and dancing of my youngest's movements and conversation, their whole being focused on building up to their announcement. My youngest sounded of water charging up a hose, of birds rustling awake clearing their throats for their daybreak glorias, shimmied with the intense, stuttered tension of paint touched just before it's dried.

Then it happened. Patrick had been carefully herded out by a close friend for a drive to the beach, and it was temporarily just the two of us—my youngest and me.

"Mum," youngest said, fingers bloodless and clenched. "I have something to tell you. Can we talk?"

Forgive me, universe, for I am human. "Sure," I said, "just give me one sec." *Forgive me, please, for I am human.* I went into my bedroom, into the space between bed and en suite.

Hiding? Nothing that simple. *Please,* I asked the universe, *don't have him be trans. Forgive me, my youngest, for I am your mum, and this won't be an easy road for you.*

I knew it was pointless to ask. The universe laid its forehead against mine and we sighed together. Crushed mint and exhaustion, falling rocks and silken, bumpy paperbark tangled between us.

Give me it all, universe, for these are my kids. I went back out to the lounge. Sat. Listened to the aircon hum as my youngest breathed wildly. Drowning. Our eyes met.

"Mum, I am not your son Steven. I am your daughter, Jessie."

She held her breath.

"Okay," I said. "Jessie." I tasted her name, melted the new beginning on my tongue. "Jessie."

She blinked.

I smiled at her, ignoring the trans-specific statistics roaring through my head, the nascent plots to hide her away so she wouldn't get hurt by jerks and idiots and anyone stupid enough to—

"Jessie, thank you for telling me that, I'm sure it was really hard."

My daughter, newly met, nodded, heaved a sigh, and tried to smile. It wobbled, fell into the cushions. She looked down.

"Jessie, I just want you to know—"

I paused until she looked up.

"No matter what, Jessie, I love you. I love you. I love you." Instant, utter, absolute.

My daughter smiled at me, bright and magnificent.

A few days later, I wrapped Christmas presents.

The kids were arguing in the lounge over a battle they were having in a game, and I had never been so thrilled to hear them squawk and tease each other.

"Ha, you lost again!"

"Yeah, well, you cheated!"

"Yeah nah, I don't have to cheat against you!"

A pause, another game started, more noise and teasing.

"I *won*! Hey, Ma, I won! I beat Patrick!" Jessie yelled.

More laughing argument.

"Oh," Jessie, all quiet.

Nothing from Patrick.

"Uh," Jessie again.

I'd gone to the door, ready to come out if something was going sideways.

"It's fine, hey," Patrick said gruffly after a second. "Just delete that and type in Jessie already. Hurry up, I want to beat you again!"

Under their mock-arguing, the tones of deleting and entering on a scoreboard tumbled, then came the music of the next game loading.

I walked back to the table, seeing blurry stars and tasting relief. I picked up a fat blue marker and bent over a wrapped box.

Jessie, I wrote.

It's been over a year now, since that Christmas. That beautiful ugly, all tied up in tinsel and worry, what-ifs and what-nows Christmas. We made it through, laughing, grouching, arguing, and with multiple time-outs on everyone's part. My kids are both here, alive and well, weird and wonderful. They know I love them, no matter what.

I love me, too. I have known the words that best fit for barely a handful of years, but never have I ever been straight. I'm demi-pansexual and hadn't sung that hymn to myself in over a decade.

So why not tell my kids I'm queer? A hundred thousand reasons held in one. Most trees don't share airspace. Slow frame rate footage shows canopy shyness, how adjacent trees adjust so each gets their time to stretch, grow, soak in air, rain, and sun. Trees that don't share? They're parasites. Or they fight for their chance at sunlight, water, sustenance, warped by those close enough to touch.

I will give my kids their moments of stretching higher, wilder, deeper than ever before. I will not steal their moment in the sun, their connection to what is manifesting in their lives, that fleeting, fragile moment that they might gift me to witness.

I can sing my own song, anytime I want.

Yesterday I found more paperbark, this piece long enough to cover my forearm. It's summer again, the cicadas and kookaburras yelling at the sunset. Jessie's on a date, soon to start university. Patrick's laughing every time I see him, excited for the future. I brush the bark's feathery edges against my lips as I look at my new calendar, then consider downloading the dating app again. I think about the boxes I will and won't be choosing. Love is love is love.

In bed, later, I'm thinking. Remembering. Maybe even dreaming a little. I hold the paperbark towards the lamp, trace the grooves and edges. There are tiny holes in the paperbark I hadn't noticed earlier that, in the quiet shadows of my room, now flare into constellations.

On Cleaving

Kerry Spencer Pray

19

Here is a secret: both my husband and I are gay.

That this is still a secret to so many people has been less about shame—though, we're Mormon, so, yeah, there's shame—than it has been about practicality, a sense of bafflement about what, on God's earth, to do about it.

Being in a mixed-orientation marriage is not something we would ever have chosen on purpose.

But in our very, very, Mormon world, being gay was just never an option. It was so far outside the realm of something we'd even *considered* possible that by the time we accepted it for what it was, we were married with children, our lives inextricably entangled.

It was too late to ask ourselves what we had done.

My ancestors crossed the plains into Salt Lake City with teams of oxen and handcarts; being Mormon is more than a religion to me. It is who I *am*.

And last year I sat in my bishop's office to discuss leaving the church.

The room smelled like my childhood. The walls were upholstered in burlap, the floors covered with industrial carpet, pictures of Jesus on the wall. The bishop tried to be kind. Tried to understand my reasons.

"I just—" I struggled for words and I didn't struggle for them at the same time. Everything I wanted to say was just below the surface, and I had clamped down on it out of reflex, knowing there are things you are not supposed to admit out loud. "Keeping the commandments," I said, "doing the *'right'* thing. It has hurt us. It has hurt us irreparably."

"I don't understand," he said. "How could keeping the commandments hurt you? Couldn't you explain a little more?"

There was a sour taste in my mouth. I felt like if I were to speak, it would fill the room. How do you explain what it means to find yourself in a position utterly in conflict with your fundamental biology? How do you explain what it feels like to *know* in your heart you are not intrinsically *wrong*. That your ontology isn't a mistake to be sorted out in the eternities?

I might have opened and closed my mouth a couple times before I spoke again. I know the room felt small. There was the bishop's face, the warmth of my husband's hand in mine, and the things I didn't feel like I could say.

I don't remember what my response was. I know I did not tell him I wasn't straight. It was none of his business, I thought. Or at least, it was not something I wanted one of my Mormon leaders to know; certain lessons are ingrained too deep.

The comfort I got from my husband's hand seemed an odd contradiction to the reason we found ourselves in that room.

But all of it is a contradiction.

That we were in this marriage at all? Because of the church. Being Mormon has hurt us more than I can say with words.

And yet, our marriage, troubled as it was, our children, as caught in the middle as they are, both of those things have brought us joy. The church has brought us joy and it has brought us meaning and it has utterly destroyed us.

The paradox lies at the foundation of all of it.

Here is something I learned from the Mormons: contradiction is the foundation of mortality.

In the Garden of Eden, there were two commandments: one, don't eat the fruit; two, multiply and replenish. Mormons believe you couldn't have done one without breaking the other. All of mortality, all of "God's work and glory" is, thus, founded on a double bind—a cleave as old as humanity itself.

In other words: it was a setup from the start.

The day we got married has a joyful sort of hazy quality in my memory now. I remember blue flowers, smiling so much my face hurt, and feeling a deep sense that I was doing the right thing.

There was a moment, right before we went into the sealing room of the temple. We found ourselves, dressed in our temple clothing, facing each other, waiting to be called inside.

The chairs we sat in were utilitarian, upholstered in the same rough fabric you find in Mormon Church buildings everywhere. He sat on one side of the hallway, I sat on the other. We looked at each other, and then I looked at the exit sign. *It's not too late to run,* was the teasing message I sent as I smiled at him.

Both of us laughed. We didn't want to run. This was written in the heavens, we thought. He took my hand then, too.

When I first found out about my husband, I didn't believe it.

Things were hard then, for lots of reasons. He'd been laid off. I'd been having a series of cancer surgeries. It seemed the worst possible moment for such a revelation.

I remember sitting on the edge of the bathtub and staring. I stared at the cracks in the linoleum, like they were metaphors. The room was cold, but I didn't shiver. I was at a loss. Not long before, there had been a thief who broke into our basement and stolen copper pipes, flooding the house and causing $20,000 worth of damage. I'd thought *that* was when I reached the breaking point.

And it was. Because that day, sitting in that room, I was beyond it. I was hovering in the nearly comical nether space of everything being just *too much*.

But the more mixed orientation marriages I've seen, the more I've found the breaking point is often like that.

There are burdens you can shoulder and pain you can bury. But you can only do it for so long. The birth of a preemie, the disability of a spouse, the loss of a child, when the challenges of mortality become overwhelming, you just *can't*. Not anymore. The very cells of your body cry out for the love and comfort they were *built* for. Something as deep inside you as prayer tells you the emptiness you have always felt and couldn't always name, the hollow sense of something missing. There is a solution for it and there always has been.

We are, all of us, God's creatures.

We can only fight that for so long before we can't anymore.

Sometime after I found out about my husband, someone in my family sat me down.

I hadn't told them about it.

I hadn't told anyone.

I'd written an anonymous essay that I published online. That was all. I'd be shocked to find out they'd seen it. (Not that they would have recognized it as me even if they had.)

The floor was slightly dusty with the debris of children running in and out of the house, the echoes of their laughter contrasting with the seriousness of the conversation. I remember the leather chairs being sticky beneath my thighs.

"If either you or your husband are secretly gay," they said, "you had better keep it to yourself."

I couldn't tell if they said it because, on some level, they knew. Or if they were just talking to talk. Certainly they didn't know the things I knew. They couldn't know how their proclamation would shape the next few years of my life.

The door slammed as my kids ran through again. They were wearing swimsuits and they left wet footprints as they ran, smeared with mud and bits of grass.

"Those are your children," my family member said. "Those are your children and they are the most important thing. Any selfish desires, any carnal urges . . . they do not matter. You can just suck it up and you can make it work until they are grown. Then, whatever. Do what you want. But you *cannot fail them.*"

I remember thinking there are more ways to damage children than by telling them the truth. I remember thinking there is always a way to help them through transitions. I remember thinking love can't be reduced to carnal urges. That there is nothing wrong with children knowing that love is complicated. That life is complicated. That we make mistakes and the very act of making mistakes was always just as much a part of God's plan.

But I don't think I said any of those things.

I'm not sure I said anything at all.

I was a BYU student when I fell in love with a woman for the first time.

I'm not sure I recognized it for what it was. Or rather, I did, but whenever I did, I shut down the thoughts hard and fast.

Instead of love, I called it friendship.

It was always a lie and I knew it. But that's what I called it.

Once, my car broke down at her house. It didn't occur to me I could have someone fix it. So I stood there on her lawn, staring at my car, and I said out loud, "I guess I need to go to the auto-parts store?"

It was twilight, the mountain air thin and cool as the sun set. I could hardly see her face in the half light.

She didn't sigh or suggest I call a tow truck. Instead, she broke into one of the biggest smiles I've ever seen. "We are going to fix it ourselves?!" she said. "This is so cool. Let me get my purse and I'll drive."

I remember looking at her, baffled to see her so giddy in the nearly dark. It might have smelled like newly cut grass. Her laughter echoed from within and without, around me, through me, nearly a part of me. I remember thinking that when I was with her, it was always joy and it was always laughter. I remember thinking it was miraculous that something that *should* have been stressful ended up being one of the most laughter-filled things I'd ever done in my life. I remember thinking it was the most sacred of mysteries: how a relationship with one person could so completely change everything for the better. I remember thinking that it shouldn't feel wrong. That it *didn't* feel wrong. That I *should* be thinking it was wrong and yet I couldn't. Because there was something pure and true about it.

I loved her more than I'd ever loved anyone or anything.

How could that be wrong?

Here is another thing I learned from the Mormons: discerning your way out of the double bind is the *point* of the double bind. When they asked Jesus what the most important laws were, he did not equivocate. Love God. Love your neighbor. On this hang all the laws and the prophets. When there is a conflict between two commandments, you are, always, supposed to choose the option that is the most loving.

Even when it's "wrong."

Eve was supposed to eat the fruit.

Nephi was supposed to kill Laban.

Any decision favoring the law over love? Cannot be the right decision.

The fall of 2016, my husband got into a single-car accident and totaled our car.

When I got the call, I was sitting in a blue recliner, talking to a friend. "One thing the Christians never quite managed to teach me," my friend was saying, "is that *love* is at the core of all meaning. It is the only thing. It is everything."

My husband's voice shook when I answered; he was shrill with panic. He'd run the car off the road, all of the airbags deployed when he hit the barrier.

My daughter was with him.

Later, when the police brought them home, I remember still being in that blue recliner. I'm not sure if I really was or if the memory of getting the call somehow imprinted over the memory of him telling me about it.

"There was smoke," he said. "After we hit."

His hand was burned, stained with the chemicals from the airbag deployment. His eyes seemed glossy. He couldn't look at me.

"Lily was crying. And as I was sitting there, I was thinking, I was realizing, I wanted to die. I didn't crash on purpose. I promise. But I was there and I was dizzy. And I knew I didn't want to be alive. And I don't know if that's why I crashed."

I knew he'd been struggling. He was depressed, he was angry, and he seemed like he felt guilty all of the time.

I knew that it would happen again. Unless we did something, it would happen again. And my daughter had been in the car with him. My daughter had been with him.

The election of 2016 was a turning point for me.

My daughter had fallen asleep on the couch, holding a map of the US she'd been coloring in red and blue by state as the polls closed. I was staring at the television, texting friends, a deep ache in my stomach.

In 2008, when the Mormons campaigned for Proposition 8, I felt betrayed. Not because of who I was. But because I felt, on a fundamental level, they were choosing the law over love. That was a hard time.

In 2015, when the church came out with its "Policy of Exclusion," barring the underage children of same-sex spouses from being baptized? That was even harder, though I found it hard to be surprised.

And yet.

I still had hope. Minds were, slowly, changing. The church was starting to acknowledge being gay was not a choice and, so, not a sin. Younger people were not reacting to homosexuality with the visceral horror and shame my generation reacted with. For the first time, I knew of openly gay BYU students, openly gay people who still went to church, people who, unlike us, were not shamed into silence about their lack of heterosexuality.

During the election, Mormons had a hard time with Donald Trump. They disliked his morals, they disliked his vitriol, his bullying. He was everything that is anathema to the core of what it means to be Mormon. For a while it looked like they might even reject him. They might vote for another candidate.

That gave me hope, too.

But as I tucked a blanket over my daughter, wondering how I was going to explain it all to her when she woke up, as I took away her halfway colored map and smoothed back her hair, I felt something inside of me break.

We, all of us, we want to do what's right.

That is what makes choosing the law so tempting. So easy. Because there is an answer and no one is going to say you did something *wrong*.

Choosing the law is easy.

Choosing the right is not.

Just before my husband moved into our basement apartment, officially marking our separation, he sat nearby as I took a bath.

The intimacy of it was nearly inconsequential. We had been together close to twenty years. We barely noticed such things anymore. Even the breath of awkwardness coming from the impending end of our marriage couldn't change that.

"Do you think," he asked me, "you'll ever date another man?"

The water around me was cooling, the smell of shampoo skimming the filmy surface of the water.

I laughed, I think. It seemed the most natural response. "The only men I have ever *really* been attracted to have ended up being gay."

(I had been so relieved when I found my husband because—*finally!*—a man I like who isn't gay! And: well.)

He might have shrugged. A few months before he had said, "I'm sorry. I'm sorry I didn't tell you I was gay before we got married. I *knew*, but I don't think I *knew*."

I could have said the same—I knew and didn't know all at the same time and I was sorry. But I'm not sure I did.

"You might find a straight guy you're attracted to?" he said. "We were really young when we got married. And totally inexperienced. You might have better luck."

I think I shook my head. My wet hair felt heavy against my shoulders. "I'm too afraid to date a man," I said. "And more than that, I don't particularly *want* to. It just . . . it seems like a recipe for heartbreak."

His face was more serious than I expected it to be. "Did I break your heart?" he asked me.

My words were clumsy, they seemed to catch one on top of the other. "I am heartbroken," I said. "But it is not your fault. None of this is your fault."

I should have been able to choose to date women when I was younger. He should have been able to choose to date men.

I said, "We did the best we could. We always did the best we could."

He nodded without speaking.

Here is something I learned from cancer: you cannot stop your body from screaming. We have this arrogant idea how we respond to things is always a choice. We say, *I cannot help but feel pain, but I can choose what I do about it.* This is wrong. When the pain is bad enough, it does not matter: you will scream.

Once, my doctor was removing staples from an infected graft. The room smelled like rotting flesh, the wound seeping with fluids.

When I screamed, I saw it hurt her. I saw her face, grim and white, trying to concentrate even though she was overwhelmed by it. I tried not to call out. I tried to stay quiet, to swallow it back, to keep my pain from hurting her.

I couldn't.

I screamed and screamed and only stopped when I started to lose consciousness.

It was not the first time this happened. It was not the last.

I spent weeks in the burn ICU and lost a quarter of my skin. I lost myself to the screams more times than I can count.

The loneliness of being a gay Mormon: it is harder than that.

None of us can escape our biology. We are all subject to the primal forces that drive our cells to cleave, our lungs to breathe.

Only God knows where the line is—knows what is and what is not a choice.

The rest of us just have to forgive ourselves. And the people who hurt us.

When we were deciding how to come out, we went to see a family therapist named Harriet. She was not a small woman, but her voice was soft. She was Black, she was queer, she wore thick glasses, and she laughed with her whole body.

"Telling my parents will be the hardest," I told her. "They are very Mormon."

My husband said, "You just need to do it. Rip it off, like a Band-Aid."

"I don't want to do it wrong," I said.

"Should you do it in person?" he asked.

"Absolutely not. They would hate that."

"I don't know. I think it shows respect."

"They would hate it," I said again. "They need to be able to take it in privately, respond privately."

Harriet sat quietly, watching us talk back and forth, not saying anything.

"I've thought about just publishing this essay somewhere," I said. "Sending them the link after it's published."

"That would be dramatic," he said.

"Too dramatic," I said. "And also, I don't want to out you, and my essay definitely outs you."

He shook his head. "Don't worry about *that*," he said. "I give you permission to out me."

"What if I didn't tell my parents about me right away? What if I threw you under the bus? Said, 'Steve is gay.' And when they freaked out I could be all, 'It's OK, I'm gay, too.'"

We both laughed.

But Harriet wasn't laughing.

I looked over at her, and her eyes were full of tears. "There is so much pain underneath this," she said. "I can *feel* it and it's overwhelming. But the way you love each other. It's beautiful. You can build whatever kind of life you want to. Being a family doesn't have to end just because your marriage has. Your family can look like whatever you want it to. And fuck anyone who says anything different."

When my husband and I were dating, we once found ourselves, after hours, alone in the Tabernacle, listening to Clay Christiansen practice the organ. It was something of an accident—we really weren't supposed to be there.

But Brother Christiansen couldn't have been kinder. He invited us over to the organ. He let us *play* it. We were alone in the Mormon Tabernacle, with the Choir's organist, and we *played the organ*. It was magical.

That space. That sweet moment. It is tainted now.

It is difficult to put into words how much all of this has hurt me. How it . . . *broke* something in me.

As I sat in my bishop's office that day, trying to explain it to him, the chair I sat in was uncomfortable. The desk between the bishop and me just another symbol of a fissure that had become too deep to heal.

"What do you think," the bishop asked me, "about Jesus?"

I wanted to tell him Jesus would not have rejected me and my husband. I wanted to tell him Jesus would never have put us in this position. I wanted to tell him Jesus would throw over the tables of the church in admonition.

All I said was, "Jesus taught us to choose love."

It is the only thought that keeps coming back to me, again and again, even now. *Jesus taught us to choose love.*

I often find myself thinking about the beginning, now that things are ending.

The day I first spoke to my husband felt like it was orchestrated by a hand that wasn't mine.

We were competing against each other for a scholarship to Oxford and we were at Utah state finals. I was coming out of my interview, keyed up and needing to talk to *someone*. He was an hour early for his (maybe the last time he was ever early to anything—which I always took as another sign of divine intervention). He was sitting in a wingback chair, light from the window beside him slightly backlighting his face, and as I came out of the interview room, he looked up at me and he smiled.

It's hard to describe what happened in that moment. It was like some fundamental part of me recognized some fundamental part of him. I knew, somewhere deep, we were the same. He was my family. And I knew it from the moment I first saw him.

Even knowing how things turned out . . . Maybe *especially* knowing how things turned out. I still feel like we were meant to find each other. I still feel like our lives were always meant to be entangled. We were always meant to cleave to each other, even as we were always destined to be cleaved apart.

If you are gay and you are Mormon, your options are painfully limited. You can be celibate. Or you can stay in a mixed-orientation marriage.

This is the worst kind of double bind: neither option is a loving one.

Because while my husband and I have always loved each other, either one of us forcing the other to stay? It runs counter to that love. Either one of us deciding the best option is to be alone forever? That runs counter to our love. Humans are not meant to be alone. And the statistics for marriages like ours are bleak.

I don't know how to be anything other than Mormon. Leaving the church was like asking me to reject my own hands, my own deepest self.

The last day I went to church was Christmas Day.

I knew I was leaving. I knew it was the last time. I wore black trousers to mark the end of my membership in the church that had thus far defined my entire life and I wore a rainbow bracelet, to mark the beginning of what came next.

My husband and I sang with the choir that day. I don't remember what we sang. I know it was beautiful. I know I felt an ache, beyond the place of words.

The choir director wore a rainbow ribbon, protesting the way homosexuality is treated in the church. It made it harder to leave in a way—because *hope*—but it also served as a physical reminder the reasons we were leaving were real.

It is hard to know what to do with them—both the Mormons who made staying in the church so impossible, and the ones who kept us hoping for so much longer than we should have hoped.

Because they were once my people.

And now I have no people.

All I have are my secrets. And even those, I am slowly leaving behind.

Essays on Shame, Suicide, and the Closet

III

Introduction to Part III

Kimberly Anderson

I am an expert in shame, guilt, fear, the closet, and suicidality. The next section of essays you will read will share with you various writers' experiences with the aforementioned topics. Please be forewarned. There are heavy, significant content warnings included in my message to you who may proceed—particularly for the essays which deal with suicidality directly ("Closed Casket," "Lynette's Story," and "By Their Fruits Ye Shall Know Them"). Please do not take this warning lightly. Even in this introduction I will speak to things that are harmful to the individual and have caused unmeasurable damage to the queer community within Mormonism at large. How can I make such a claim to be an expert in shame, guilt, fear, the closet and suicidality? Well, my trauma dossier is strained with receipts. I am a queer, transgender woman, raised in an orthodox Mormon household. My adopted parents both come from the venerated "pioneer stock." There is a heritage of obedience to church leaders that we honor and revere in our family. Hovering parents and extended family believed in an eternal chain of celestial proximate bliss that would be broken by any disobedience to family or church. To deviate from strict obedience from family or church meant certain disapproval from hovering parents and extended family whose spiritual and religious beliefs meant that you were breaking an eternal chain of celestial proximate bliss.

In queer space we speak of The Closet. What the fuck is it? Well, I can only speak to my reality.

The Closet, for me, was constructed out of walls that we will label ignorance, naivete, isolation, and a heavy sliding door of solid twenty-four-karat shame. There was no ceiling. I could look up and see blue sky and fluffy clouds. Inside the closet it was vast and bleak. It was wallpapered with question marks that would make The Riddler envious. It was dim. It was a cul-de-sac of misinformation. A faint glow of the outside shone through the razor-thin gap beneath the bottom of the Door of Shame. Distant voices could be heard just barely above my heart's quickly beating pulse that was an ever-present pounding in my eardrums. This closet began to be built slowly around the age of eleven for me because it was at this point in my life I was beginning an understanding that my inner gender dissonance was continually drifting further out of tune. I was seeing that who I knew I was would not be welcomed warmly by my family, my church, my own self, or the God that I was taught to believe in.

My closet was to be a place of continual questioning into a vacuum that was void of any meaningful answers. I did not see it as a safe harbor, yet it paradoxically offered me tremendous safety. I believe if I had been aware of more information about who and what I was, it may have been too much for me to handle given the immovable religious positions I found myself occupying. If I had known, if I had seen but a glimpse of an authentic life that was indeed possible, then knowing it would be eternally out of my reach could have pushed me to a space where I would have wanted to shuffle off this mortal coil prematurely.

Two things saved me from ending my own life. First of all, I did not know how to successfully load the hunting rifle that my adopted father kept. I wasn't sure if the bullets he had would fit in it. Not fully understanding how it worked, I was afraid if I had tried, it would most certainly end in a nonfatal mishap, the end of which I might never fully physically heal from. There was a much worse fear, however: I was terrified that my adopted mother would never let me emotionally escape the shame of a failed suicide attempt. It was this not knowing how to operate this particular lethal weapon, combined with the shame that I feared from the very woman who chose to adopt me, that kept me alive.

Several years ago, while still attending graduate school in California, I traveled to the site where a young, scared, and gay Mormon boy named Stuart Matis decided he needed to simultaneously send out a very direct message of harm, as well as end his journey of pain. This was where I was to make the first photograph in an ongoing series documenting sites where LGBTQ members of the church had decided they would die by suicide.

I knew that Stuart had died near where I was working in the San Francisco Bay area, and I did a little research and learned that his life ended at a stake center in Los Altos, California. I traveled there, read his last letters to family and friends, walked around the site and exposed a few negatives. It was the first, and last, image I have made in that series.

My path to becoming a therapist has taken me through some inner journeys that are as painful as they are healing. They are crucial in developing my ability to work and sit with clients in their own unique pain. I have had to continually confront my panoply of inner and external demons. One of those demons is suicidality.

I have read and heard numerous accounts from straight Mormons who had very strong thoughts about suicide and dying before the age of eight years old. These people had thoughts as children that if they died before they were baptized that they would automatically go to Heaven. A strong and common thread among them was death by suicide prior to turning eight years old. These are the thoughts of straight and cisgender Mormon children under the age of eight. Kids who by all other accounts are welcomed and celebrated within Mormon culture. Kids who still felt the crushing fear produced by doctrinal guilt and shame without the additional stigma of an alternative gender identity or sexual orientation to be concerned about. Occasionally, but more often than we would like to admit, that eight-year-old child will gradually get older, discover their own gender incongruence or attraction to people of the same sex, and sometimes both. By the time they are young adults they have been saturated with messaging from the church that being gay, lesbian, bisexual, transgender, or anything other than straight and cisgender is a tragic, sinful character flaw. One that will keep them from joining with their family in Celestial Glory for the remainder of eternity. Occasionally, but more often than we would like to admit, that individual finds the burden of being queer too much to bear and decides that it is preferable to die at their own hand than to live a life of shame and guilt, stigma and judgement, fear and self-hatred. Occasionally, but more often than we would like to admit, that person who leaves their life early and unfinished gives us clues after their death as to their motivation and reasoning.

I have spoken to members of law enforcement who respond to unattended deaths and have heard numerous graphic accounts. These stories often involve canonical LDS young adult books that were required reading up until just a few years ago. A former prophet has written arguably one of the most emotionally damaging books in the history of the Mormon Church. Spencer W. Kimball's treatise on repentance titled *The Miracle of Forgiveness* has been present at many sites where individuals have died by suicide. Often the book is open to Chapter Six, which is titled "Crime against Nature." To cite any passage or page number is to give it too much credit.

None of that book is true. All of it is false.

Sadly, myself and countless other queer Mormon youth took its pages as literally the word of God, largely because by the time we were reading it, Spencer W. Kimball was actually considered the living prophet of God. How dare we have any thoughts contrary to it? Many could not reconcile the two positions and have found themselves in a battle where their flesh would ultimately succumb. Many parents today rely heavily on the foundational understanding of homosexuality and transgenderism that they processed and learned from within the erroneous pages of that book.

As a mental health clinician working with many hundreds of Mormon and former-Mormon LGBTQ adolescents and adults, I can state without hesitation that guilt, shame, and fear are the tools that have damaged them repeatedly both at the hands of their parents and also at the hands of the Mormon version of God. Many of these people have been injured by the practice of "Reparative Therapy" at the hands of ill-informed practitioners armed with the Spirit of God. I have heard stories from people who attended BYU and were coerced into these heinous and harmful "therapies," quackeries and snake-oil, in an attempt to change and hide their sexual orientation or gender identity.

Queer people are among those who the Mormon God has decided are expendable. There is no definitive doctrinal place for us. The Plan of Happiness leaves us very, very sad.

Research regarding Mormon queer youth done by Dr. Brian Simmons indicates that 73.4% of LGBTQ people raised in the church heard strong, damaging language, and impacted them emotionally enough that if a diagnosis for PTSD was part of the research, it would be given to them.[1] Just by requiring our youth to sit in the pews, we are unwittingly inflicting significant trauma on them. Year after year, decade after decade. I know that this is true. I took Dr. Simmons' survey. I am part of that 73.4%.

In the following several essays you will hear messages of shame, guilt, fear, trauma, many closets, coming out, and death by suicide. You will read of those who made it through the pain, and those that were unable to. If you, or a loved one you know will be emotionally activated by the following essays, please take a break. Breathe deep. Go outside and look at the sky. Take off your shoes and walk in the grass. Drink some water. Go for a walk. There is no hurry and no obligation to finish. Please take it at a pace that is healthy and beneficial to you.

If you are finding yourself alone and emotionally distraught, please reach out to the National Suicide Prevention Lifeline at: 1-800-273-TALK (8255). If you are trans or nonbinary, please call the Trans Lifeline at: 877-330-6366.

Please know that if you are a queer Mormon or queer former Mormon, or anywhere in between, that you are exactly as you are supposed to be. You are the perfect creation of the universe and have no need to be changed by anyone else. You can be authentically you and stand firm in the knowledge that it is exactly there, in our honesty, where we do indeed find lasting happiness.

NOTE

1. Brian Simmons, "Coming out Mormon: An Examination of Religious Orientation, Spiritual Trauma, and PTSD among Mormon and Ex-Mormon LGBTQQA Adults," (PhD diss., University of Georgia, 2017), 78.

Closed Casket

V. H.

20

I first saw her in the restroom in the Harris Fine Arts Center, the HFAC, at BYU in 1978. I was washing my hands during a break in my music theory class, and another girl came out of a stall and began to wash in the other sink. When she tugged the sleeves of her red hoodie up to wet her hands, I saw her wrists, wrapped in heavy gauze bandages, and I stared a bit. She didn't look up at me, but she knew I had seen, and there was an almost physical jolt of shared shame: unerasable intimacy, reluctant and apologetic and embarrassed and intense all at once, and I was grateful for the sound of the water echoing on the tile walls, making talk not impossible, but not likely. The moment passed, but we both knew. I also knew I was not—could not be—content letting her go with that one complex, impacted encounter.

After class we found each other in the hallway, the stream of indifferent students jostling us closer to each other until we spoke. I do not remember how the conversation started. But we ended up sitting in a practice room playing music for each other and with each other—duets we'd both learned, and hymns everyone knows, and then improvising piano four-hands, giggling until we were breathless. We kept talking after they closed the HFAC, and we were still together hours later, walking and talking and getting hot chocolate at a restaurant almost three miles away from campus.

"When I was nine," she said, moving her spoon in the cup of chocolate, whipped cream melting into the cooling dark, "my mom died. Cancer."

I did not say anything. I looked into my own cup, dregs of chocolate and cinnamon in the bottom.

"We lived in Jersey, and they wanted to start busing that year. My little sister and I would be going to a school basically in the projects. My mom was always sort of sick with something, but as she got worse, as the chemo got worse, it felt like she took my dad away, too, you know? Like they were both gone. And I had to get my sister on the bus every morning, every afternoon when we came home.

"And the school was so much worse than the one where we lived. Just down the street. And some neighborhood kids' parents—got them out if it. Somehow. Got them out of being bused."

She put down her spoon and took a sip. Held the cup in both hands, so I couldn't see her mouth as she said, "And there was this one day, on the bus home. I told my, my sister. My little sister. I told her, 'You know what? Sometimes I wish—sometimes I wish she would just get it over with.'"

"'And die. At least we'd have dad.'"

"And you felt guilty—but it's not your fault, it wasn't your fault—!"

She shook her head. "You don't get over it though. I know I'm not magic. But that was the day, the exact time."

She sighed and tugged her sleeves back over the awkward bandages on her wrists. "That's only one story. I got lots!" She flashed a humorless grin. "Lots of stories, lots of reasons. You don't get over it. No matter how many shrinks tell you."

We stayed to close the place.

When we were back near her dorm, it felt easy and perfect to hug her goodnight. And she didn't let go. And I didn't let go. We stayed in the embrace for so long I forgot everything else. We held each other as if it were death to let go. Because it was. Because, even when I was her friend, her best friend, her roommate, the enormity of love was too much and not near enough, and she fought the demons and she continued her dark romance with blades and pills.

Denial doesn't feel like denial. It feels like integrity.

That summer she stayed with me and my family a few towns over, since her family was overseas. And that fall we were roommates in the dorms. She wasn't movie-star beautiful, but there are, and there were then, actors that look like her.

I married a boy when I was still a girl. The fall when she was my room-mate, I got engaged, and every day of the engagement, at age eighteen,

I swore to myself and to God that I would not break up today. Today, I was not going to be a disappointment to my parents like my sisters and their divorces—five divorces among four sisters: not me. I had integrity. I had made a promise, and I would be keeping it.

I lay awake across the room from her one night, crying, sobbing, grieving, terrified, not knowing why I felt such overarching dread of an unknown, horrific future, and horror of the loss. I yearned for a day not long before I met my fiancé, the familiarity of walking alone in the rain—and I would never have that again, never be myself again—I knew it, somehow, but I could not find the explanation for that loss. I just knew my life as me was over before beginning, and that I was losing that solitary walk and that rain forever.

She woke up. "What's wrong?"

I could hardly speak for sorrow, for terror, for the dryness in my mouth, for the spectre of my life ending so early, and my marriage beginning so soon. "I don't want to marry him. I don't want to get married at all, and I am scared to death. So scared." And I fell back into silent heaving sobs. She sat up in her bed. "It's ok, it's good. Your kids are his. I've seen them. And I've seen the world if you don't marry him, and it's wrong, but if you do, it's right. It will be ok. It will be ok. It will be ok." She calmed me and brought me back to myself, away from that terror, and I slept that night. And in a way she was right. It was ok, in some senses. I did marry him. I had his children. But I was right to be terrified. But she was also right to calm me.

Before Christmas, but after classes were over, I was packing up to go home. I moved some boxes out from under my bed; did not find what I was looking for and slid the box out from under her bed. When I pushed her notebook aside, I found two razor blades underneath it. I had not recently looked closely at her hands and arms. But it was winter, and long sleeves and long pants could cover bandages she would have applied herself. I did not confront her. I had written a piano sonata for her, and I gave it to her, dedicated to her for Christmas, with a note that said, "Please love yourself as much as this music loves you; please, please, hear in this all I tried to put into it for you." Sometimes in the years to come, when she wanted to reach me, to bridge the distance imposed by time and society and expectation, she would play the theme, or hum it, so that I could hear it. Whistling it when I was slow waking up in the morning. Fiddling on the piano in the Relief Society room when she was playing the prelude or postlude; once or twice leaving it as a wordless message on an answering machine, our code. For something. We never did say what.

She married, too, years later, when I already had a child. One of the children she had seen. Her groom was starkly blond, and tall, and very quiet. Her marriage was annulled over three years later, he having come out to her on their wedding night. She tried. Like I tried. But he was gay; my husband was not. I had children. She had a PhD in social work, and she taught students and clients about suicidal ideation and how to bring despairing souls back to themselves.

Late in the winter of 1989, I got the message that she had died. It was late at night and my husband and I returned from a concert. I paid the babysitter, checked in on my sleeping children, and saw the blinking light on my telephone. She had been missing for four days, and a search party had found her body at the bottom of a ravine in the Smoky Mountains. About a hundred feet above, there was a poorly maintained trail, and there were days-old footprints in the dusting of snow. The footprints only headed one direction and disappeared above where she was found. They said she had fallen. They said there was evidence she had clung to the brush around the spot where the trail had given way in the thaw and freeze and rethaw of the season.

I flew across the country for the funeral. I don't remember it except that her family was devastated, but stoic. And no one called it suicide. Her one-time husband was not there. But I was.

It was a closed casket.

A Conversation I'll Never Have

Jasper Brennan

21

"Hey, Dad. Can I talk to you?" I would ask, stepping nervously into his home office. My stomach would be in knots, but my mind would be firmly made up—no turning back.

Sure, he would say, or maybe, *What's up?* He'd swivel his chair around to face me. He would know it was serious from the tone of my voice and the directness of the question.

"I have something I need to tell you," I might say, trying to force my breath to come normally and my body to stop fidgeting.

Ok.

There would be an empty seat, but I would remain standing. I would take a deep breath. I would stumble over my words.

"I know you've been worried that I'm gay," I would begin. "I mean, you've asked me a few times, and I know you've asked some of my siblings, too, in case I told them in secret." He would be frozen at this point, terrified that I was going to confirm his suspicions.

"I'm not gay, exactly," I would continue. "Have you ever heard of asexuality?" He would shake his head. "It's a sexual orientation, just like gay or straight. So, if you're gay," I would explain unnecessarily, "you are sexually attracted to people of your same gender, and if you're straight, you are sexually attracted to people of the opposite gender. If you're asexual, or *ace* for short, you don't experience sexual attraction to anyone. And that's what I am."

I would watch my dad's face carefully. *What does that mean?* he would ask, and I would ignore the fact that I had just given the definition.

"It means that I don't experience sexual attraction. Not all aces feel the same way, but for me it means I'm not interested in sex at all." To be perfectly clear, I would add, "Even after I'm married, if I get married, I have zero interest in ever sleeping with anyone."

I can't decide how he would react to this. When their daughters are young, it is every dad's dream that they will stay away from boys for as long as possible, and the way he sees it, I'm still his little girl (he doesn't know that I never really was that little girl—that I am, and have always been, nonbinary—but that's a conversation for another day). Then again, my dad has expressed concern about my lack of dating multiple times.

Maybe he'd say, *You just haven't found the right person yet.* Or maybe he wouldn't respond because it would feel too awkward. Either way, I would press on, because there would be so much more to say.

"It isn't about finding the right person. It isn't a phase or a defect. Being ace is just part of who I am." My stomach would turn as I transitioned to the next phase of the conversation.

"But just because I don't experience *sexual* attraction doesn't mean I don't experience *romantic* attraction," I would say, searching for, and finding, hints of confusion in his face. "I want a romantic relationship—the emotional intimacy, the commitment, love. I just don't want it to include sex."

Maybe I would pause here to let him speak, but probably not. I would want to get the next few sentences out before I lost courage. "I'm biromantic, which means I'm romantically attracted to people regardless of gender," I'd say, the words rushing together, "I am attracted to people based on their personalities and their intellect and how it feels to be around them. What gender they are doesn't really matter."

Now I would be silent. My dad would take a deep breath or two. *It matters to the church,* he would say, or something similar. *Obviously, you can't get married in the temple if you want to do . . . that.*

"I know," I would say. "I mean, I disagree with the idea that it's a sin to love someone of your same gender. I think that there's a lot wrong with the way the church deals with its queer members. But I know that, as it stands, me dating a woman goes directly against church teachings."

Whether you agree or not, it's still a sin.

"I don't know," I'd respond, wondering whether I should have just nodded and stayed silent. "I think maybe we got it wrong."

I think the Family Proclamation[1] is pretty clear. At this point, his eyes would narrow and his lips would curl back into the forced, mirthless argument smile he puts on when he expects disagreement. It isn't a happy expression. It's more like a dare. *Disagree with me*, it challenges. It expects to win.

I wouldn't wear an argument smile. My armor is bright eyes and a firm voice.

"I think the Proclamation is influenced by cultural norms and expectations," I would say, eyes bright, voice firm. "General Authorities are human, too. They have biases and make mistakes."

Not like that.

"Paul did," I would challenge. "He said women shouldn't speak in church. That wasn't the gospel—it was a cultural expectation."

Men and women are made to go together, my dad would say, ignoring my argument. *Men with men or women with women—it's just unnatural.*

"Actually, lots of other species in nature engage in same-sex mating."

It doesn't matter what animals, or even people, do—it matters what they are supposed to do. It's just wrong—you can't even have kids that way.

"So, the only point of having sex is to have kids?" I would feel fairly confident for a moment as I continued, "That would mean that any time two heterosexual people slept together and used protection, or if one or both of them were unable to have kids and they still had sex, that would be wrong."

That's not what I'm saying, he would argue. *It can also be a way for a husband and wife to grow closer.*

"Then why not a husband and husband, or wife and wife?" I would stop there, remembering his reaction the last time I brought up nonbinary gender identities. That would have to wait.

Because God said so.

I could keep going, could talk about how just because God placed Adam and Eve together as the first parents doesn't mean we have to follow the exact same pattern, how there are nontraditional family units in the Bible and in Mormon history, how even if "gender is an essential characteristic of individual premortal, mortal, and eternal identity and purpose,"[2] that doesn't necessarily mean the way we understand gender is correct. Maybe I would say those things, and more. But eventually, I'd rein the conversation back in.

"This isn't even relevant," I would say at some point. "I told you, I'm asexual. I don't intend to have sex with anyone anyway."

His answer would be something to the effect of, *That won't always be the case,* to which I would most likely shake my head and roll my eyes, because I've heard it so many times. *What about kids?* he might ask, assuming this proves his point.

"I don't want kids," I would say, and feel a rush of adrenaline. This, too, is taboo.

You say that now.

"Even if I end up wanting kids in the future, I'll adopt," I would say before he could finish his thought.

His lips would tighten into a thin line. *What if your husband wants kids?*

"Well then he probably won't be my husband, will he?" I would say this lightly, as if it were comic relief, but neither of us would laugh.

You aren't likely to find many men who will be okay with that—with any of this, my dad would warn. I would be prepared. I think about this often.

"I know," I would say. "But I would rather be alone than with someone who would try to pressure me into doing something I'm not comfortable with." This language would give him pause. Maybe he would begin to understand—not that I am asexual, because he probably wouldn't believe it to be a legitimate orientation, but that this is something I feel strongly about.

Let's talk about the bisexual thing, he might say after a moment.

"Biromantic," I would correct.

Is this a new thing? Are you dating someone—a girl? Where did it come from? His argument smile would be back, if not overpowered by a smirk of disgust. *I'm just trying to understand.*

"It's not new," I would answer, unable to address all his questions at once. "I've only recently admitted it to myself, but this is how I've always been. I just didn't want to accept it before."

Because you know it's wrong.

"Because I've been made to *feel* like it's wrong. But I'm thinking for myself now, and I don't see what's so wrong about it. I used to feel *so* guilty every time I thought about women. I told myself that I wasn't actually attracted to them because I didn't want to have sex with them—I couldn't be homosexual or bisexual because I wasn't *sexual* at all. But still, some part of me wasn't convinced. I guess that part of me knew that romantic and sexual attraction don't have to be connected."

Well, I'm sorry if I did anything to make you feel like you were a bad person. I hope you don't think I set out to make you feel guilty. I wouldn't be sure whether to believe him or not. I wouldn't answer.

By now, he would be getting antsy, ready to end the conversation. *You know what the church says about same-gender attraction,* he would say. *I can't condone what you're telling me.* He might shrug to further indicate that the situation was out of his hands.

"I know," I would say, because, no matter what I might have hoped, this is the response I would be expecting.

He would have one more concern to address before ending the conversation.

Are you going to keep going to church?

How to answer? Yes, because my testimony of the gospel still stands strong, even as my testimony of the institutional church wanes? Maybe, because the local ward seems accepting, or because I'm straight-passing, so they don't care? No, because I'm tired of queerphobic policies, casual slights, and feeling out of place?

"I plan to try," I would say. "It's getting harder and harder, but I believe that Heavenly Mother and Father accept Their queer children as they are, and that, if church leaders are receptive, They will guide us in the right direction. And if it gets to be too much, emotionally, I'll stop going, and it will be hard, because I'll be separated from something that has been a major part of my life. But ultimately, my relationship with my Heavenly Parents is the most important thing, and I feel strongly that They are rooting for me."

My dad would nod, not in agreement, but because the conversation would be over. I'd slip out of the office after a few moments of silence, once it was clear that neither of us had anything else to say. I'd head back to my room feeling unsettled and uprooted, even though I know he wouldn't kick me out or disown me or anything so drastic. I would wonder what he thought as I left him alone—would he be caught up in the shock of having a queer child? Would he be angry or disappointed that I had come into my own and was unwilling to change to fit his expectations? Or would he reflect on what I'd said, and try to understand? Would he remember how I had said with confidence that my Heavenly Parents were on my side, and then feel a pang of regret when he realized I couldn't say the same of him?

These are questions to which I will most likely never know the answers. The closet is a tough place to be, but, for the moment, it seems to be the only option. Occasionally, I peek out through the slatted doors or the gap at the floor, or prop the doors open to show my true self to a trusted friend. But for the most part, I live here, in this cramped, dark enclave, waiting for a *right time* that may never come and a hand that may never be extended.

So, hello from the closet. I may be invisible, but I'm here.

Waiting. Hurting. Praying.

Maybe, reaching for a handle?

NOTES

1. Known colloquially as "The Proclamation," or "The Family Proclamation," the document titled "The Family: A Proclamation to the World" was created by the church in 1995 specifically as a legal document to combat the normalization of same-sex relationships and argue against same-sex marriage on moral grounds. It places heterosexual monogamous families as central to the Mormon faith.
2. "The Family: A Proclamation to the World," last modified September 23, 1995, https://abn.churchofjesuschrist.org/study/scriptures/the-family-a -proclamation-to-the-world/the-family-a-proclamation-to-the-world?lang =eng

Out/Into the Closet

Anonymous

22

On February 19, 2020, the LDS Church unveiled their new General Handbook with expanded policies limiting transgender members. Later that same after-noon, BYU appeared to lift its restrictions on same-sex dating, a move which quickly eclipsed trans issues in the media. This vignette was written the day after, on a long bus ride home, as a picture on my phone stirred up emotions I didn't even realize were there. A week later, BYU would rescind its approval of same-sex dating.

Yesterday, a group of queer BYU students ventured into the Honor Code Office to confirm whether the removal of homosexual behavior from the Honor Code meant they could date, hold hands, or kiss without fear of reprisal. They were told they could.

Eager to spread the news, they posted jubilant selfies on social media, smiling alongside BYU employees and sharing a kiss under a statue of Brigham Young. A wave of emotion rushed through me as I recognized the freedom and relief in their eyes. *That's how I feel when I kiss my wife,* I thought. *That sense of rightness.*

And then came another wave of emotion, because while so many of my friends just found a path out of the closet, yesterday brought the news that my wife cannot use her name, or her pronouns, or wear the clothes she feels best in, without incurring "restrictions on her membership." I spent the rest of the day in a daze, joy and sadness overwhelming my heart in equal measure, all the while unable to explain to anyone why I'd had a reaction to these photos at all. I knew they'd say,

"Well, I don't see why this affects you. You've always been allowed to kiss your husband."

The Ocean That Shaped Me

Abby Kidd

23

Every summer until I was eleven, my family camped on the Oregon coast. We spent our nights in a tent and our days on the beach. My dad took my brothers and me out into the freezing water of the Pacific Ocean, all the way out to where the waves broke. My dad's hand clasped mine as we moved farther and farther out, and my body tightened from cold and anxiety as the waterline crept up past my waist. White foam obscured my view of what lay beneath, and my imagination filled in the spaces with every possible danger—jellyfish, crabs, unspeakable monsters. The water pushed and pulled, threatening to sweep my legs from beneath me. My dad stayed right there, close enough to make me feel safer in the deep, rushing water. Once chest deep, we turned around and dove forward with the crashing waves, letting them carry us toward the outstretched sand. After my legs went numb, the cold was bearable, and we'd stay out there bracing against some waves, swimming against others, and riding a few all the way in to shore until with chattering teeth and blue, salt-parched lips, we walked back up the beach. My mom waited there to wrap me in a towel. I learned early that the ocean was powerful and unpredictable. Maybe that's what made it so inviting. Three out of four of us seafarers were queer, though that word and its ramifications were unknown to us then.

As a tween, I moved with my family from the Pacific Northwest to southern California. We didn't have to wait for a vacation to go to the ocean anymore as it was a short drive from our new home. We were used to barely being warm enough to don swimwear at the beach, but here our skin turned pink in minutes. We were old enough and strong enough swimmers to take to the waves by ourselves with our brand-new boogie boards tucked under our arms. To learn how to use my board, I watched others. I learned that you need to start catching the wave a little earlier than you think, that you have to paddle hard before it crests beneath you to make it in time, that the best way to deal with a breaking wave is to duck under it, and that sometimes when the wave is timed badly, there's nothing you can do—you're going to get tumbled hard. The first time it happened I felt like I'd entered a black hole. My nose and mouth filled with the sting of saltwater. The current twirled and tossed me, and I lost all sense of orientation. When the wave finally passed, my feet searched for firm ground. Finally I found purchase beneath me and trudged back to our beach blanket, my arms and legs limp from the effort. I sat with my forehead pressed against my knees, swigged fresh water, and went back out into the ocean wiser than I started. When my mom called me back so we could head home, I was exhausted, satisfied, and a little worse for the wear. At the same age, I watched other girls for their cues about being a Mormon teen—talk about boys, shave your legs, wear makeup, cry during testimony meeting. Don't let anyone think you are gay, "skanky," or partying.

Now, I live on an island surrounded by the emerald-green waters of Puget Sound. We don't have great big waves that smash the shores, but small ones that lap against rocky beaches. Sometimes the waves are just big enough to break. In the summers, I swim in the ocean with my daughter. When we moved here she was afraid of seaweed, squealing any time it touched her. Now we bob in the water that, close up, is clear. When we stand chest-deep, we can see all the way to our feet as if we are looking through glass. She teases me by throwing the slimy seaweed in my direction. Together we make new memories and discoveries in this water.

This ocean contains so much of me, so much of my childhood and self. It has drawn me in since I was small, and still it pulls me like a magnet, not just to see it or smell it or hear it, but to be immersed in it, to feel its gentle pressure carrying me, making me part of its powerful vastness. I don't want to conquer this undulating, immeasurable body. I just want to know it intimately, the way I know by my husband's breathing whether he is tired, anxious, or calm. I want it to stroke my skin and pull me close, to show me just one tiny part of itself; but even that part, an infinitesimal fraction of the whole, engulfs me.

In my dreams, I see a roiling sea, a little girl bobbing, waiting for rescue. She's only seven or eight and I'm worried for her safety, but the little girl is me—the reason she is different, and her fear of that difference won't be uncovered for decades.

In my dreams, I see massive, pulsing waves carrying in them giant, deformed creatures: orcas, seals, a fish the size of a whale, all dead. Nobody else will look and see them. They only want to see the sand, the blue horizon.

Mormonism is my ocean. For all its power, for all the ways it has crushed me and tumbled me, for all the times it has blued my lips and numbed me to its freezing water, I can't stop coming back to it. It is my mythos in the same way as my memories of the frigid waters of my childhood, full of nostalgia and longing. Like the sirens it calls me back, even though I know it can and will swallow me whole, its alluring promises leave me dazed.

Nearly every close friend I have is someone I met because of the church. Even my parents wouldn't have married, my birth would never have happened without it. I couldn't erase it from myself if I wanted to, though I'm not sure I'd want to. I was tossed into it as a little kid, and sometimes I just need to sit on the beach with my head against my knees, breathe deeply, and grab a sip of fresh water before I go back in. For a queer person, the water is never calm for long. Sometimes I dream of swimming to shore, placing my feet on solid ground, and walking away. But I was born to swim. My body doesn't know how to live without this water, without the rhythmic stroke of my arms and the thrumming kick of my feet. I crave the salty breezes and the shock of cold against my bare legs, but I don't know how many more badly timed waves I can weather. It has never really been safe for me here. For brief stretches I float, soaking up the sun, always wondering in the back of my mind when the next wave will crash.

I can't be angry when I am slammed against the ocean floor. My body is too weary from being churned under water, my lips too sore and swollen from the harsh saltwater, my voice too inaudible over the roaring tide. It's the ocean, after all. This is what it does.

Hard Conversations

Jaclyn Foster

24

And by the time I identified as being gay, it was too late. I was already homopho-bic, and you do not get to just flick a switch on that. No, what you do is you internalize that homophobia . . . because the closet can only stop you from being seen. It is not shame-proof.—Hannah Gadsby, *Nanette*

The LDS Policy of Exclusion leaked the first Thursday in November, 2015. I learned about it via Facebook. And on Friday, November 6, 2015 at 3:50 PM, I came out of the closet on Facebook.

The first thing my mom said was that she was angry at me. Of course, she loved me, and she accepted me, but she was angry that I hadn't given her a heads up, that she'd had to learn about it on Facebook at the same time as everybody else. It was a valid complaint, but when your brain has been on fire for over twenty-four hours straight, anger is not an emotion you're equipped to deal with. Because of all the adrenaline muddying my brain, I don't remember anything about that conversation, except that I was crying, and she was crying, and she said she hadn't known what to tell my sister.

"She's fourteen," I said, "I think she can handle it."

"Not about you. About the policy."

Three years and a lot of unspoken conversations later, I get it. My mom wasn't any more prepared for the Policy of Exclusion than I was, and for your child to suddenly confront you with hard questions you can't answer is a lot to handle. My mom said my sister was mainly concerned about the children, and how hard it would be for them, and the conversation contained a lot of "I don't know," "I hope so," and "we'll have to show them extra love and pray for them." It was an unsatisfying resolution, but I think she did a good job.

And yet, three years later, that's the part of my coming out story that's stuck in my head. Not the part about me, but about my sister, and being fourteen, and having hard conversations.

When I was fourteen, it was the end of 2007. I had a fake crush on a guy I knew was just a friend, and a real crush on a girl I thought was just a friend. Gay marriage had been legalized in Canada before I could remember it, but in my heavily Mormon province, Proposition 8 loomed large. We didn't phone bank, or donate, or speak much about the proposition per se—my parents couldn't even remember if we were supposed to support Yes or No—but the topic swirled around me. General Conference. Seminary. Even in my public high school, the combination of Mormon students and the Canadian fascination with all things south of the border meant that social studies and English discussions regularly came back to it.

My parents didn't have a hard conversation with me. In fact, we didn't have any conversation at all. I can remember exactly two times my parents discussed homosexuality with me, and both were by accident.

The first was when I used our appropriately public desktop computer to read a blog by a faithful Mormon "struggling with same-gender attraction." I didn't know we had anything in common, but I read post after post, glued to the faith-promoting shame pouring out from between the pixels, when my dad walked in and asked what I was doing. His face crinkled in disgust as he said, "Don't read that stuff." I was confused. The anonymous author was going to extremes to *keep* the commandments, but the blog was still "that stuff"? The shame kept me from asking any more questions. I just nodded and closed the window.

The second, a few years later, came as we watched season one of *Modern Family*. Cam and Mitchell shared a kiss onscreen, and I froze in shock. They did it like it was so normal. Just like anyone else kissing? Was it allowed to be normal? Was I being homophobic *right now*?

What was I supposed to do?

My mom looked at my carefully composed face with concern. "Maybe we shouldn't watch this anymore. It normalizes this too much." It wasn't allowed to be normal.

The shame-based conversation vacuum was readily filled anyway. Conference talks, Sunday School lessons, and heated debates in Social Studies 10-1 where I quoted Leviticus, all in quick succession.

I kissed a girl, and I liked it played as I suntanned. I repented and turned off the radio.

"Your analysis of Katy Perry's music is so unbiased even though you're Mormon," my English teacher praised.

Baby you were born this way. I repented and turned off the radio.

"Love the sinner, hate the sin," my seminary teacher explained. Of course. It was so simple. Why would anyone think Mormons are homophobic? I updated my Leviticus-based argument accordingly.

"This assignment is so hard. I haven't been able to find any secular sources about why gay marriage is bad for society," my BYU classmate complained. "Have you found any?" I shook my head silently. What if there weren't any?

My mission companion reached for my hand, innocent comfort after a long day. "Haha, wouldn't it be awkward if I were a lesbian?" I joked. She laughed, too, then got mock-serious. "But Sister Olson, it's okay if you are." I laughed again, sure this was still part of the joke. She snuggled in closer, oblivious to my racing heart. It never occurred to me that she was actually serious.

I don't know. I hope so. We'll have to show them extra love. Hard conversations I never got to have.

So I wish, when I was fourteen, someone close enough to me had caught my mom off guard so we could have a hard conversation. Because by the time I came out, by the time we started having hard conversations, I was already homophobic.

25

Lynette's Story
Kerry Spencer Pray

When I see her in my head, as I saw her that first time, she is slightly back-lit, slightly bowlegged, with her slightly masculine round face, standing in her too-tall athletic socks, her black hair falling wild around her shoulders. We had both arrived to play intramural basketball for the chemical engineering team and we were outnumbered.

"There are two of us!" she said, looking at the way we were surrounded by only boys.

"Thank goodness," I said. "I'm bad enough as it is. I wouldn't want to make *all* girls look bad just because I can't play."

"Oh, I am not very good, either. They really shouldn't expect much of our team."

I remember it was cold and it was dark and by these things, I guess it was late fall or early winter. It was on the first floor of the Richards Building and the echoes of sneakers squealing against the basketball court were so vivid I can still nearly smell the sound. I was seventeen years old. I had dropped out of high school the year before to come to college early and it was my first year at BYU.

"It doesn't matter to me if we win or not," she said.

"Good," I said. "Because we probably won't."
She laughed and it was loud.
Lynnette always laughed loud.

It has been about twenty years since I last saw her, spoke with her, or heard her laugh.
All of my memories of her are conditioned by that.
I can see her, sometimes I can nearly hear her voice. I am not sure about any of it anymore. Not even the parts of the story I thought I knew at the time. Over the years it has only become clearer how much I didn't understand.

Once, after a game, she said, "We should go somewhere." Maybe we'd won, maybe we hadn't, I don't remember. "To celebrate." She was grinning. She did not look you in the eyes when she grinned, she always looked away, as if even—maybe especially—happiness was not something you were ever supposed to fully share with someone else.
"Where should we go?" I asked her.
"Somewhere with food. Hamburgers. Ice cream. I can drive."
I remember she had a muscle car, but I didn't know anything about cars, let alone muscle cars, so maybe it was just something sporty. It was red, or maybe it was brown. We drove through the dark, our T-shirts damp with sweat, shivering and looking out the window. I remember seeing stars. I don't remember how far out of town we had to drive to find them. We listened to Chicago. I knew she was older than I was, and the way she sang along with the lyrics, I decided she must be much, much older than I was, even though she was an undergraduate, just like I was. But who can say? I sang along with the lyrics, too.

Once, I remember Lynnette, struggling with a television.
"You didn't have to bring your TV here!" I laughed at her, as she set it down on my dorm-room desk. My roommate Rebecca was lying on her bed, eyebrows askew.
"We needed a movie night!" She was unrepentant.
"We could have *gone* somewhere," I said.
"Sure, but, you know. Here we are? I also brought snacks."
My roommate Rebecca sat up then. "What snacks did you bring?" she asked.
Lynnette's pockets were stuffed, overflowing with Ziploc bags. "All sorts of snacks," she said.
I remember I thought of hugging her, but I stopped myself. I stopped myself because once she had reached out for me, as if she wanted to hug me, and she had pulled herself back, quickly, and completely, and with a

finality. It was in this way I understood: Lynnette was not someone who you were supposed to touch.

I accepted this, even if I never thought to question why.

One night we sat overlooking a part of campus we called the Ruins. They were overgrown, terraced as if they used to be part of a stadium. I don't know if they ever actually were. They were hidden behind some faculty offices, a secret place.

"Are you going to one of those dances this weekend?" I asked her.

If she laughed, it was silently. "I don't go to dances," she said.

"Why not? What's wrong with dances."

"There are boys at dances," she said. "And they might, you know, want to *dance* with me."

"You don't like boys?"

"Not particularly."

"None of the dances look that good anyway," I said. "And they're all off campus somewhere. It's easier when things are on campus."

"Our Tribe of Many Feathers Club," she said. "I'm Navajo, have I told you that?"

I don't know if she had.

"We're having a big party in a few weeks. There will be dancing and there will be Navajo tacos, which are possibly my favorite food."

She paused and she looked at me. She looked at me for maybe too long. And then she looked away.

"You should come with me," she said.

We moved in together at the end of winter semester. An apartment, just south of campus. It didn't have a dishwasher and, in the fall, six girls would have to share a single bathroom. That summer there were only four of us, though. She sat on the porch some nights, fixing an old bicycle, her bag of tools spread around her in a circle.

The Utah Jazz were in the championships that season. At night, we would make dinner and we would watch basketball.

Whenever I laughed, she would look at me until I noticed she was looking at me and then she would look away.

She came into my room once, holding a tape recorder. "Hey," she said. "Can I . . . Can I ask a favor?"

"Depends on what it is," I joked.

"I'm supposed to make a meditation tape for one of my classes. I wrote up a script." She waved a paper. "Would you read it for me?"

"Like on tape?"

"Your voice," she said. "I don't know. It's just soothing."

I laughed. "Literally no one has ever told me my voice is soothing." My voice is deep, nearly masculine. It has a throatiness to it where words sometimes get muffled.

"Well, *I* think it's soothing. Listening to it would help me sleep."

I nodded. Neither of us were particularly good sleepers.

"Sure," I said. "I'll record some tapes for you."

The script was about what it would be like, being welcomed back into heaven. That the pain would be over. The struggle would be over. She would be made perfect and whole.

Sometimes I still think about that.

About how it was in my voice.

One night, I got home from school late.

The door to our apartment was open, debris was scattered from inside out onto the porch.

"Hello?" I called, tiptoeing into the apartment. "Is anyone home? Hello?"

Lynnette's bicycle was turned upside down next to the couch. There was a row of cherry pits, lined up on the edge of the kitchen table. Tools were scattered everywhere. Clothing was on top of the television, dishes were turned upside down on the carpet.

I stood in the doorway when Lynnette appeared, arms waving, looking at the wall and laughing. "Peaches hunt at midnight," she said.

"They what?" I asked.

"Yellow dance up with a fox?"

I just looked at her.

She picked up one of the cherry pits and put it in her pocket.

"Are you okay?" I asked.

"Mugthought akemp." She laughed again and turned back to the table.

I snuck past her, taking the phone off the wall, and I called 911.

I rode with her in the ambulance. She kept standing up, sitting down. She laughed as they took her blood pressure, she laughed as they asked her questions. She laughed for no reason at all.

"How long has she been like this?" they asked me. "When did it start?"

I shook my head. "I don't know," I said. "I just got home. She was alone."

We were in the emergency room for hours, most of which was me trying to keep her from leaving as she became more coherent and wanted to go home.

Imaging eventually found she'd had a ministroke, cause uncertain, and she was admitted.

My aunt drove me back to my apartment.

Sometimes I wonder how things would have been different if I went immediately to bed when I got home.

Would I have finished my engineering program? Would I have taken a job as a resident assistant? What about her? What would have happened to her?

But I didn't go immediately to bed.

Lynnette had given me a list of things she wanted at the hospital, and I wanted to bring them to her.

It was one in the morning and I was bleary with exhaustion. The carpet seemed to hold my feet to it as I went into her bedroom.

She wanted her tape player, music, and she wanted her meditation tapes—she couldn't sleep without them. I reached onto a shelf she'd built out of particle board and stacks of concrete cinder-blocks, four to a shelf. I set aside the tape player, I pulled off a box of tapes and I sat down on the floor, back to the improvised bookshelf.

I'm not sure what happened.

Maybe I bumped the shelf. Maybe I'd destabilized it when reaching for the tape player, when I removed the box of tapes to sort through them, maybe she'd done something to it when she was having the stroke. I'm not sure the whys or hows matter.

The bookshelf collapsed, a dozen cinder blocks falling as much as six feet down, hitting the back of my skull one after the other, and burying me beneath a mass of particle board, concrete, and debris.

The girl who found me and dug me out estimates it was several hundred pounds I was buried beneath. I don't know if that's right, but it certainly isn't wrong.

I was flown out of Utah a couple days later, my neck still braced. I needed to be watched for longer term effects of a brain injury and my parents lived in California.

I didn't talk to Lynnette that summer. (I didn't really talk to anyone that summer.)

I lay in a dark room (the light hurt) at my parents' house, head propped against pillows, neck needing to remain braced for weeks.

When I went back to BYU in the fall, I had trouble concentrating, I had headaches, math seemed so much harder than it used to. I dropped all of my engineering classes for the semester. Eventually I dropped out of the program entirely.

I had taken a job as an RA on campus, so Lynnette wasn't my roommate anymore and, since I'd dropped our shared classes, I didn't see her anymore.

She could have reached out.

She did not.

I could have reached out.

I did not.

Sometime the next winter, Lynnette called two young men from her ward and she asked them to drive her to the hospital. While she was there, she swallowed an entire bottle of antidepressants.

They were unable to resuscitate her.

Sometimes I still think of her.

I think of her holding a plate of Navajo tacos. I think of her singing loud, with her window down, Chicago and starlight.

It is only pieces. Broken pieces, skewed by memory. But Lynnette can't tell her story.

And the pieces are all that are left.

By Their Fruits Ye Shall Know Them

Jodie Palmer

26

I wrote a suicide note today.

Holding it in my hands felt like a terrifying relief. Will you belay me by wrapping these words around your waist and setting your feet to witness me?

I excised everything and everyone from my life that might compromise my effort to live as a straight woman—people, places, things. I invited in everything and everyone that should bless and heal me—a husband and children, scriptures, prayer, fasting, temple worship, service, and sacrifice. And yet, I suffer bitterly.

To all the suicide prevention advocates who remind us not to ascribe a single reason to a suicide, that there are so many nuances and elements to a person's story—fuck you. My story won't be watered down with "nuance" and "elements."

I have one reason for wanting to die. I am stuck. I can't live as a heterosexual woman for one more second, and I cannot bear for my family to pay the terrible price of this. This is my bitter suffering. I'm so tired. I am desperate for the pain to stop.

At twenty-three I found myself in the desert, without family or friends, with virtually nothing but the clothes on my back, sitting white-knuckled in my new bishop's office. I described to him the shame that I had loved a woman, that I had been expelled from Rick's College for it, that I had wanted to marry her but I'd abandoned her instead and had run to the farthest, most desolate place I could get myself to. I was sorry that I could not find a way to run fast or far enough to escape this terrible evil that ever followed me. This evil that was me.

His eyes sparkled, and his grin spread wide in response. He almost laughed with the simplicity of the solution. "Jodie, all you need to do is date. This is what I want you to do, and everything is going to be okay. This is absolutely resolvable. Don't you worry a bit."

Was this hope true? He was so confident in the solution, and I was desperate for that confidence. My relief was profound.

Surely, he'd handed me a good seed, and I planted it. I watered it. I dunged it. I pruned it. I cared for it with all the effort of a faithful servant in the vineyard.

Alma 32
41 But if ye will nourish the word, yea, nourish the tree as it beginneth to grow, by your faith with great diligence, and with patience, looking forward to the fruit thereof, it shall take root; and behold it shall be a tree springing up unto everlasting life.

3 Nephi 14
17 Even so every good tree bringeth forth good fruit; but a corrupt tree bringeth forth evil fruit.
18 A good tree cannot bring forth evil fruit, neither a corrupt tree bring forth good fruit.
19 Every tree that bringeth not forth good fruit is hewn down, and cast into the fire.

Twenty-six years later, I am harvesting the fruit of a tree that is all wrong.

It bears the good fruits of children and marriage—patience, humility, sacrifice, service, selflessness, support, ministering, comforting, change, growth, charity, vulnerability, unity, safety, and joy.

It also bears the evil fruit of silence, bitter suffering, and wishing for death.

Tell me, is this a good or corrupt tree? By which fruits shall I know it? And, shall it be kept or cast into the fire?

This is the terrible paradox. This is cruelty revealed, down to the white bone.

What should be done with this intractable conflict?

I pick the fruits and swallow them whole, seed to stem, like a wild-starved prisoner. The seeds mingle and I wait, wondering what tree it will be that springs up from this planting in the depths of my own soft belly.

27

Way in the Closet, Serving the Lord
Judith Mehr

I am a well-known artist in the Mormon community and have received numerous commissions to paint portraits of LDS General Authorities, produce illustrations for church curricula, feature Mormon values and lifestyle by depicting scenes of everyday life in paintings now hanging in a variety of locations owned by the church.

I grew up in the LDS Church, attended BYU, graduating with a Bachelor of Fine Arts degree in 1974. Subsequently I spent twenty-six years painting artwork for the church on commission. During that time, I also worked with the church art conservator helping preserve the church's historical art collection, cleaning and restoring artwork in the Salt Lake Temple and Museum of Church History and Art.

About halfway through that twenty-six–year period I discovered that I was a lesbian. Okay, I didn't just discover it then. I finally *accepted* this discovery that I was a lesbian, because I had always had inklings of this knowledge about myself, never acting on it when I had previously felt attachments to others. I was finally ready to accept it at a time when I met someone with whom I fell deeply in love and was forced by this discovery to confront this issue head on.

The journey of accepting my sexuality in the context of believing myself to be a beloved child of God was excruciating. There was lots of prayer, lots of reviewing of personal history to see where things had veered off course, lots of wondering how I could possibly be "one of those!" I had always had an extremely strong sense of self-worth and belief in my mission as a servant of God, growing up with a conviction that using my talents to further the work of the Lord was what was required of me and for which I dedicated myself with all of my heart. But, now, how could I view myself? How could I be this beloved servant of God and also be homosexual?

I tried to understand the societal preconception I had that I would now be referred to as one of the lowest types of human beings on the face of the earth, having to claw my way back up, by fasting, prayer, scripture reading, sackcloth and ashes (flogging, scourging, wailing, gnashing of teeth, etc., etc.) just to get to the level everyone else (heterosexuals) was on and then somehow be "changed" by these efforts back into heterosexuality.

Somehow, throughout this self-discovery process, an amazing thing happened and I could never *feel* this "condemnation" in my soul (even though I tried to feel it). I could never believe that I was "that bad!" This image of me as a horrible being with this horrible condition just wouldn't root in my soul as a description of myself! Subsequently, the answer came strongly and clearly to me from the God I knew and loved: Heavenly Father *loved me just as I was* and, furthermore, instructed me to remain in Salt Lake City with my new love, instead of fleeing to remove myself from temptation!

For twenty-seven years thereafter, I was with my partner. We were both severely "in the closet" while I continued my painting career with the church. We attended our ward together. I helped her raise her four children in the church, the oldest boy eventually going on a mission to the Philippines. She was a divorcée, going back to school to become an elementary education teacher. She finished her degree and got a job as an elementary school teacher, where she has been teaching for 22 years. We lived in separate houses, two blocks apart, so as to maintain an illusion of "just friends" to the outside world.

We lived in a ward that was a bit suspicious of any single woman ("oh, married women, watch out for the predatory single woman who will steal your husband!") At times I felt that we were both viewed somewhat curiously by the Relief Society ladies. My own quirkiness of personality, liberal artsy attitude, and bits of masculinity were initially met, as I began attending this ward, with suspicion. Later, I was finally accepted when members found out I was that "Judith Mehr," the famous church artist whose work was gracing their curriculum media materials.

Both of us held various jobs in the church. I went around giving lectures, showing slides of my church-related paintings to various missionary groups, ward groups, stake groups. I had many wonderful experiences with ward members who became friends. My partner and I felt that we could actually pull off our fabrication of lifestyle successfully, even though I was finding that being duplicitous about my behavior was causing me a lot of personal pain. I was "Aunt" Judy to my children. They did not know about their mother's true relationship with me. She continued to date men occasionally in order to maintain the correct "picture." She never wanted any of our true relationship to be known by her family, friends, or school colleagues. Eventually, I came out to my own family. They knew that my relationship with my partner was very positive for my own life happiness and accepted me. My partner could never tell her family and we continued "in the closet," with her family and friends, for our twenty-seven years together.

While I accepted myself as a lesbian personally and privately, I did not know how to maintain a closeted deception indefinitely. I longed for some sort of acceptance by the church because I knew I was accepted by God, so why couldn't there be some acceptance and answer from the Brethren about it? I did propose marriage to my partner, even though I knew that wasn't legally possible at that time. We exchanged rings as a symbol of our personal commitment to each other, even though we could never acknowledge this to the outside world. Our personal discussions as partners were never able to find a mutual solution in bridging the distance between fear of discovery and living truthfully in the open as a couple.

In the early '90s, I was asked by the church to paint a portrait of Apostle Howard W. Hunter[1] for the church's Museum of History and Art. When I entered Elder Hunter's office to meet and photograph him for this portrait, I was met by the most intense feeling of perfect love and acceptance directed straight at me coming from this man. It was overwhelmingly positive and so personally fulfilling that I could hardly talk. I have met many General Authorities during my painting career, painted portraits of several prophets and apostles, but this meeting was incredible and I knew I was accepted and loved, both by Elder Hunter as a representative of Christ and by God. The photos I took that day provided me with a bit of that glow from his face that I was able to capture in the portrait I painted of him.

Later, when he became the prophet for a short time, I fantasized that he would institute some form of marriage for homosexuals. Maybe he would make a special ruling or something, or get a revelation that would provide a way for us to be in pairs as eternal partners. I had felt his love and I knew that it was possible. He was only the prophet for eight months, passing away suddenly and unexpectedly. But I knew he was spiritually way out in front of all of the rest.

Little by little, sometime in the early 2000s, the deception and pain, doctrinal inconsistencies, and cultural misogynistic issues began to take their toll on me and I chose to become inactive. I continued painting for the church from time to time, but those commissions became less frequent and I didn't aggressively pursue them. My partner continued in her church activity for a while after I left, but slowly she also let her activity go as the children grew up and went on their way. It was so much *less* painful for me now not going to church, although I missed the singing of hymns and the spirit of worship. I knew that I still had my relationship with Heavenly Father. I knew that He loved me. I knew that He would continue to direct my paths. I knew that it was OK with Him that I take myself out of that pain and constant reminder of the impossibility of melding the church with my life issues.

So, I moved on in my mind, always having a backward glance at what was happening in the church, paying attention to any hint of change, any outrage of action against homosexuals (Prop 8), any possible signs of softening. Meanwhile, gay marriage became legal nationally! I thought that maybe, finally, I should now actually get married. Then, after thinking, along with the rest of the Utah gay quasi-Mormons, that after the public nightmare brought to the church from the Prop 8 debacle, the church was softening up a bit by assisting in passing legislation in the Utah Congress that included civil rights protections for gay people, the church slammed the door shut on our hopes with the November 2015 policy change pronouncement. Such horrible thoughts began running through my head, knowing that to be considered an apostate was the most egregious of titles to be applied to a member of the church. My first inclination was to hide again, get back deeper into the closet, forget about the marriage idea altogether. I became fearful that if the church found out about my double life that somehow all of my paintings, my life's work and contributions to the Lord, would come under scrutiny and possible removal. I was really distraught. Furthermore, I knew that tender young LDS people who were discovering their gayness would be in danger of hopelessness and have possible suicidal thoughts. Indeed, after a very short time, the suicides started mounting up.

After discussing my feelings with my partner, a number of gay friends, and some of my relatives, I decided to reverse my fearful course and publicly "out" myself to the Mormon community, using my artwork and modest fame to draw attention to the possible tragic unintended consequences that this policy change was going to cause. I wrote an op-ed[2] that appeared in the Salt Lake Tribune on January 30, 2016, essentially imploring the LDS community to love their gay children, relatives, and friends and, at the same time, revealing my sexual identity to this group.

Fortunately for me, this action has not produced any backlash that I am aware of. My paintings are still in their places, as far as I know. I have been welcomed and embraced by many Mormon friends and relatives. The policy has caused extreme distress for countless souls! It has also made it quite clear to me that I have been discarded, like a dirty old rag, from a society that I once believed truly wanted to become like Christ. I, however, continue to love and honor Jesus Christ. I consider myself a Christian in the truest sense, embracing all of God's children.

It was entirely freeing and personally gratifying to "out" myself! Since that time, I have allowed more of my true personality and feelings to be expressed, finding immense strength and purpose in new painting images and activities. I still watch "the church" and follow the "one step forward, two steps back" faltering progress, or lack thereof, of church actions. I wish them well. There is great potential there for positive humanitarian assistance and action, if they would only heed the call to love, include and, indeed, embrace, *all* of God's children.

NOTES

1. Howard W. Hunter was an apostle in the LDS Church from 1959 to 1994 and the president and prophet of the church from 1994 to 1995. His brief tenure as prophet included the drafting of the Family Proclamation, which was released after his death.
2. Judith Mehr, "As LDS grapple with handbook change, know that God loves his gay children," *Salt Lake Tribune,* Jan 31, 2016, https://archive.sltrib.com /article.php?id=8208202&itype=storyID.

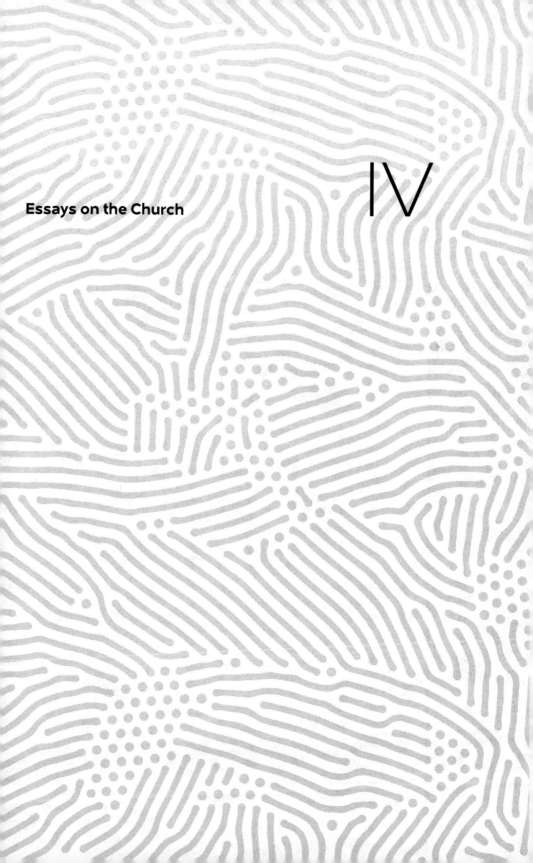

Essays on the Church

IV

Introduction to Part IV

Taylor Petrey

What does it mean to be a queer member of the Church of Jesus Christ of Latter-day Saints? There is no homogeneity in any of these categories, which is the very thing that makes these coexistent identities possible, but more often irreconcilable. Regardless of one's particular identity, it seems that it is a question we find ourselves fascinated by and experience a deep urge to tell these stories and consume them. Why? Is it because we tend to see a conflict between two competing identities, queer and Mormon? Is it because these competing identities are so often experienced tragically? Is it because a listener finds words for themselves paradoxically in the stories of another?

There is no single answer to these questions. Stories grounded in lived experience draw on a particular kind of knowledge, often based in trauma, conflict, and discovery. These stories are raw with emotion, sometimes hopefulness and love, often fear and uncertainty, but more often just searing pain and hurt. As many of these writers explain, the conflict between being Mormon and queer is both the source of fascination and frustration. So much of the way that the writers featured here tackle this question is also to complicate what it means to be trans, queer, lesbian, or bi, and also what it means to be Mormon.

In order to understand that conflict, and how many of these writers experience it, one needs to know something of the historical, social, and political context in which modern Mormonism has come to exist.[1,2] What it has meant to be a Mormon in the past several decades is to dwell in a deeply heteronormative environment that the church has deliberately cultivated. Mormonism certainly exists in a broader heteronormative culture, in the United States and beyond. At the same time, the church has specifically worked in preaching, politics, and psychological circles to denormalize same-sex romantic relationships and kinship.

While Latter-day Saints share such beliefs with a broader conservative religious network, there are also distinctive ideas that guide how many Latter-day Saints understand gender, sexuality, and sexual difference. As an expression of these beliefs, in 1995, LDS Church leaders issued "The Family: A Proclamation to the World," which expressed a belief in male/female marriage alone, as well as an "eternal gender." Such teachings motivated church actions and established a church culture that opposed same-sex kinship and trans identities.

The Proclamation, as it is known, also contains a reference to "Heavenly Parents," a distinctive LDS teaching that supports a heteronormative church culture. In this theology, God the Father is married to a divine Mother—together they are the Heavenly Parents to humanity. There is a genealogical relationship between humanity and divinity, sometimes in the most literal of senses. In such teachings, heterosexual, reproductive relationships are ideal in part because they reflect the divine model. At the same time, this understanding of God often entails an intensely personal relationship. More than an abstraction, this paternal God is an active participant in the lives of devotees, which can amplify the intensity of the love or feelings of rejection that many in these stories recount.

Among the teachings that inform these stories are the beliefs about the progress of life, including a premortal life and a post-mortal life. This present life is neither the beginning nor the end of one's journey. An expression of LDS belief, this understanding of the eternal nature of the human soul also tends to contribute to beliefs that trials in this life may be remedied in the next. For this reason, some of these stories discuss a contemporary LDS teaching that one's errant same-sex attraction may be "healed" in the next life.[3]

In addition to the teachings, something of the structure of church life is needed here to fully understand these stories. There are frequent references to bishops, missionaries, zone leaders, Relief Society, Young Women's and Young Men's, Sunday School, seminary, and more. These are all titles and terms familiar to insiders who navigate the various organizations and positions of authority. Often, these are gendered organizations. The priesthood is restricted to adolescent and adult males, which divides all members of the church into binary gender roles and often hierarchical gendered authority. Women's organizations exist and women do have some authority in certain contexts, but the formal authority is maintained by male leaders appointed to positions of leadership. Missions structure many of these stories. A rite of passage for many young Latter-day Saints and an intense emotional and social experience, missionary service often pushes individuals to their limits and beyond, and missions often occur during the developmental stage in which many young adults are solidifying their identity.

While these teachings and structures have a great deal of influence on LDS practitioners, they cannot be considered determinative for how many Latter-day Saints navigate their own personal identities. Latter-day Saints exist in productive tension with the broader social context in which they exist. In his classical sociological study, Armand Mauss describes the quest for "optimal tension" that groups must achieve so that they are not so different as to be exiled or irrelevant to broader culture, or so similar that there is nothing distinctive about their identity and claims.[4] This is all well and good when describing social group dynamics, but how this plays out in individual lives is yet another thing.

One of the things that these narratives illustrate in vivid terms is how this conflict between the church (its teachings, culture, and leaders) and many of its members taxes that relationship so heavily. As the church has pursued a heteronormative agenda, those who do not fit such norms can experience extreme pressure to conform. Suicidality is one of the ways that some attempt to cope with the tensions that the stigmatization and ecclesiastical discipline to enforce these norms produces. Many experience it as a form of social rejection and a threat to their eternal happiness. At least in one account, such enforcement came in the form of physical violence. That "tension," when sought, is often created on the bodies and lives of those at the margins. Optimal tension for the group as a whole often means horrific tensions for subgroups within it.

When answering what it means to be a queer member of the Church of Jesus Christ of Latter-day Saints, these stories illustrate what it means to exist where one's body, desires, and identity are at the center of a cultural pressure point.

NOTES

1. Gregory A. Prince, *Gay Rights and the Mormon Church: Intended Actions, Unintended Consequences* (Salt Lake City: University of Utah Press, 2019).
2. Taylor G. Petrey, *Tabernacles of Clay: Gender and Sexuality in Modern Mormonism* (Chapel Hill: UNC Press, 2020).
3. Petrey, *Tabernacles of Clay*, 182–87.
4. Armand L. Mauss, *The Angel and the Beehive: The Mormon Struggle with Assimilation* (Urbana: University of Illinois Press, 1994).

28

Unspeakable

Eliana Massey

"I don't know if I believe in God, but I know I have a fear of God."

This was how the first gay Mormon friend I ever had answered when I asked if he still believed in God.

He added, "I pray at night because I'm scared of what will happen if God does exist and I don't. I don't believe, but if I don't pray, I can't fall asleep."

Three hours later, sitting in a math class, I looked down and noticed my hands were shaking. I couldn't make them stop. I wanted to ask him where he found this information about God. I wanted to find the source and destroy it. Where did this come from? But I knew. Locked inside a hundred Sunday school lessons, General Conference talks, and heartfelt prayers are seeds of terror.

The Mormon God is not kind to queer children.

I was sitting on my sandy colored carpet when he told me about his boyfriend and the shame he felt about having him. Staring out my window, I'm sure I could see cars passing by, but I don't remember them. I knew someone needed to tell him it would be okay. I'd lost every reason to believe that queer love is wrong in God's eyes, but I still wondered if I was wrong and what that would mean. What if I told him it was okay and it really wasn't? What if my spiritual discernment had been clouded over with counterfeit deception?

"Even the elect shall be deceived."

"Do what is right. Let the consequence follow."

Being wrong felt like a risk I had to take. This is what faith feels like to me.

Once, in one of the few dreams I have ever remembered, a red-haired young man stepped out of a car with a cardboard box. (Somehow, I knew he was gay.) He walked up a cement path and stopped in front of a glass door I recognized. It was the door I always used to enter my childhood church building. He swung the door open and gently placed the cardboard box, labeled "to take" with a black sharpie, by the ward library's door. From above, I could now see that the cardboard box was full of white dress shirts. (Somehow, I knew they were from a mission in Japan.) With that, he walked back out the door. As he walked back to the car, a friend poked their head out from the driver's side window—smiling. Even though the parking lot was dark, I could now see there were also a couple friends in the back of the car. The young man smiled back, hopped in the car, and they drove off. I woke up—crying. Somehow, I knew it was going to be okay.

Another time, in a dream, I watched a girl I loved sink in a lake. As if it were a levitation magic trick, she rested right below the surface before coming back up even more beautiful. I marveled at the way the water droplets stuck to her coils of dark hair. Then, I dreamed I woke up. I dreamed of my mother. "Did you have any dreams last night?" she asked. My mother asked this often when I was little. My mother believes in dreams. Her story, as a convert, starts with a dream. I almost told her my dream, but with a boy. Instead, I told her about the girl. I began to freeze up. I waited for her to wince. She looked straight ahead. No emotion rippled over her face. I figured she was trying very hard not to react. The conversation moved on. I woke up from the dream. I said nothing.

"I am sorry you have suffered."

One of the first times I opened up to someone about my experience being queer in the church, they told me this. I remember the sound of my body exhaling as if I had been carrying something heavy and finally set it down. The yellow of my walls blurred as my eyes filled with tears. It was the first time someone ever called what I had gone through, and was going through, suffering. I couldn't stop crying. Something solemn and condemning wakes in the word. The part of me that likes to keep up appearances doesn't hesitate, "Well, not really. I mean—" Yes, really. I didn't know I had suffered. At least, I never would have let myself use that word. Before I understood my own queerness, I thought I was a "horrible ally," who could never speak up because she was too afraid of anger or tears seeping through her words.

"Would you like to come out at church?" a therapist asked me. At that moment, the cobalt blue couch I sat on felt too hard to be comfortable and too soft to support my weight. My back was perfectly straight and I held my body as if I was levitating above the moment.

I opened my mouth. Shut it. What was I supposed to say? I didn't know. All I could think was, "You do not understand Mormonism."

I can't put these things into words. That's the specific color of them—unspeakable.

I Owe a Debt

Rebecca Moore

29

When I was a senior at BYU–Idaho, I was my ward's Relief Society president. I had also begun to dip my toe into the coming-out pool. At that point it was kind of an open secret, as it were, within my ward. Not so much a secret, but rather I had told some people and didn't particularly care if they talked about it. It wasn't time to get up in front of the world and announce, "I like women and I like men! Thank you for coming to my TED Talk," but I was ready to start being open. I wanted to make gay jokes that were good and talk about my crushes on girls and just be honest.

One day my neighbors down the hall made a comment about a woman being really hot on a TV show and they should go get me. All of the women in that apartment were my good friends, but one had somehow missed the queer memo. She looked up, dismayed, and asked what they meant. "Rebecca's into women. Didn't you know?"

She did not.

The next day she showed up at my door, looking worried. "Can I talk to you? Alone?" As the Relief Society president, this wasn't particularly unusual. I didn't think it would be anything more than the regular woes of a student at BYU–Idaho. We sat down and I asked what I could do for her. Her eyes had a hard time meeting mine but finally she told me that her roommates had told her about my sexuality.

"They said you like girls."

I smiled. "Yeah. I do."

"But you're the Relief Society president?"

"That I am."

"Does the bishopric know?"

"Yep. So does the stake president."

Her eyes looked at me with confusion and wonder. And then it came out.

"I'm like you. I like girls, too. I thought that I couldn't tell anyone. That I was bad."

I was horrified and spent a while assuring her that she was not bad, that she was loved, and nothing was wrong with her. Apparently the only other people who knew were her parents, who were not members but were deeply conservative evangelicals. To say that they did not approve was putting it mildly.

It was that day I realized that I needed to talk about being queer more. Not just so I could make more and better gay jokes, but for her. For people like her.

The world I exist in is not the same as others. Sometimes I refer to it as "The Rebecca Bubble." A huge factor in this is the fact that I am a conventionally attractive cis white person. Yes, I'm a woman and queer, but it would be absurd to imply that I deal with the same levels of discrimination and oppression when my life is dripping in privilege. There's another layer that I have never been able to explain of The Rebecca Bubble. People who shouldn't want to listen to me do, no one typically tries anything with me, and people (white men) who would say something objectionable become quiet when I am in the room. I tell you this not to brag, but to explain that one day I realized the world wasn't fair and the bias was in my favor. I was in my late teens when I realized that people listened to me an illogical amount. I remember thinking, "Well, better make whatever comes out of your mouth worth listening to."

That day, the woman before me was baffled that I got to float through one of the most conservatively religious schools and have people know me, know all of me, and still see my humanity. She feared, and perhaps rightfully so, she wouldn't get that same treatment. And I was again reminded that it wasn't fair. It wasn't fair at all.

But maybe if I was a little louder about my sexuality, the people around me could learn to see the respect that LGBTQ people deserve. Because if I was queer, maybe it's not so bad. Maybe people would stop for a second, and rethink what they thought they knew.

A few months later, I went out to lunch with my uncle who had come out back in the 1970s. He was now the head of the University of Maryland's

LGBTQ Equity department. At this point, I was ready to be all the way out and I wanted to talk to him first. I walked into the faculty dining room at the university, happy to see him, but still nervous to tell my first family member. He sat with a refined dignity that I admired. It was unassuming and comforting, as if to remind whoever he was with that the respect he had for himself was extended to them as well. Unsurprisingly he was supportive, but he gave me a warning. "This won't be yours anymore, even though it's about you. Everything is now going to be about other people's feelings about you being queer, not you just being queer. You'll have to be there for them during this trying time." That last bit was said with his driest tone and a small smirk. He was right, but I felt ready for that.

It wasn't just that now older white men who somehow respected me would perhaps consider the humanity of an entire group, it was that deeply closeted queer people would see me. See that not hating themselves was an option, that being happy was an option. Yes, I wanted to demand basic decency from straight people but I wanted to say what I said to that girl in my apartment to every queer person. You are loved. You matter. There is no better way to explain my motivations in coming out than the old saying, "Comfort the afflicted and afflict the comfortable."

And so I've moved into a space of education and advocacy within whatever circle I can find. And when I run out of patience I try and find more by remembering how kindly I have been educated in my own life, about trans issues, racism, classism, and so many other things I don't have to experience. I remember that those people were probably tired but they were kind to me, and hoped I would learn to be better. And some days I want to strangle people when they seem willfully ignorant about LGBTQ issues or to want to pretend like sexism is totally overblown. But good faith was given to me, and so I try to pay it forward.

Michael Lewis once gave a speech at Princeton called "Don't Eat Fortune's Cookie." In it he discusses how so most people who have quite a lot of good fortune have it largely because of luck. One of my favorite quotes is, "You owe a debt to the unlucky."

I am a very lucky queer. I am a very lucky woman. My life has not always been perfectly insulated from reality, but I educate because I am profoundly aware I owe a debt to the unlucky.

30

If I Can Find Hope Anywhere, That's the Best I Can Do

Kaja M. Kaniewska

In the summer of 2018, I was asked to give a talk in church on Matthew 5:9.[1] I've spent most of my adult life working on sustaining and reviving Jewish heritage in Poland. The idea that the indifferent are as guilty as the attackers soaked into my brain. I responded to the topic almost automatically. It was as if my heart has been writing this talk my entire life.

On a Sunday morning in Warsaw, Poland, I told the congregation a story:

"There was a young woman in the early 1940s who agreed to aid another young woman in hiding her baby boy from certain death. They hid the boy for five years. They were both his mothers, even if only one gave birth to him. Care and sacrifice defined motherhood for them.

"In Poland, we all know that the Righteous Among the Nations[2] receive a medal with a Talmud quote: *Who saves one life, saves a world entire.* We repeat this phrase so many times that, for some, it may lose its entire meaning. But for me, it's still full of sanctity: the boy those women saved grew up to be my grandpa. He created my *world entire*. And he was only able to do that because a young woman long ago decided to be righteous and save a child of a stranger."

I cried and noticed the women in the front rows wiping away tears. I wanted to leave the impression that we bring peace by caring, for example, by seeing a sister in a stranger and a son in her child. I felt I had done a good job.

Next hour, in Sunday School, I was happy and relaxed when I raised my hand to offer a little humorous remark about an Old Testament lesson. I can't even recall the topic or the words that I said. What I do remember is one man who stood and turned to look me in the eye. He then informed the room that Jews don't deserve to be alive. If I had ever wondered what it felt like for somebody's words to slap you in the face, I knew at that moment.

When I first joined the church, it saved my life. My gratitude for my Young Women's president and for my patient missionaries is endless. But I realize now that the recovery from depression also served to push me back into the closet. Or maybe I pushed myself back. My desperate wish to fit into the new community I loved caused me to bury the careful queerness of my teens.

Overcoming depression brought back the desire to fight for my real self, but the fight was slow. I already knew that church members are capable of being bullies as cruel as the ones you remember from middle school. I've seen anti-Semitism. I got into fights with condescending men.

It was never a question for me that coming out an open and proud transgender man would bring changes into my religious practice. The real problem was whether I could be genuinely religious while hiding who I am. The thoughts kept coming during the sacrament: am I honest with myself and with God? Wouldn't loving parents prefer me to come to Them as I am, as They created me?

One Sunday I put a picture of Harvey Milk into my scriptures and wore a suit to church. The world did not collapse. The peaceful feeling that came to me during the sacrament was a confirmation of the one truth I desperately wanted to know—it is easier to worship if one's not busy pretending to be someone else.

That year ward members became aware that I was on the organizing committee for Warsaw's Equality Parade. That's when I started getting the stink eye in church. Later I found out that several of those stink-eyeing members went to the branch president to suggest that I should be excommunicated or at least get called to repentance.

It was a part of what later prompted the all-branch third-hour[3] meeting. The branch president began the meeting by saying, "Some of you are coming to me declaring that this-and-this person is doing something wrong, and a this-and-that person should repent—brothers and sisters, that is a sin. You have no right to judge."

Unfortunately, I don't think that the lesson sank in.

I struggle with that one, too. Once you offend me, there's always going to be a wary little voice in my head reminding me of it. But I try, I try, and

I do feel guilty. At the very least, I keep most of my judgmental thoughts to myself. That's the very least a decent person can do.

A year later in early summer, I skipped Sunday School, again. I sat outside of the chapel, soaking in the sunshine, when a friend joined me. His child had recently come out as transgender. Their whole family had been doing a terrific job of being supportive. But seeing his child so vulnerable in this world takes its toll. I felt immediately that he came to me for comfort that day.

"How do you see yourself in the Plan of Salvation?" he asked. "How do you think you fit in?"

What a hard question for a parent. If he takes what's being taught in the church literally, one of his children won't join him in Heaven. One beloved child who's done nothing wrong.

"To be perfectly honest, I don't know. But God wouldn't create someone who would have no chance of coming back to him, would he? One thing I do know is that this is who I am, so this must be who He has meant me to be—there must be a place for me. But we don't understand yet."

"That's what I've been hoping for," he said. "That God will figure it all out in the end."

They moved out of the country just before the hell broke loose.

Later that same summer, along with some friends, I visited a small, rural town that held its first-ever LGBTQ pride march. Police in riot gear tried to contain a crowd that threw stones and firecrackers at us. The day was a blur. Pride-goers huddled in small groups. I got a tight hug from a boy I'd just met. I was rushed by emotions to help a young mother carry her terrified toddler to safety. I recall a moment when the music started playing and we danced, we sang, and then we had eggs thrown at us.

"Eggs are fine," a friend laughed. "Eggs make a great hair conditioner." Then I remembered collapsing on a train, only allowing myself to breathe deeper once we saw Warsaw's skyline on the horizon. Warsaw is safe, Warsaw is ours.

As the most experienced LGBTQ activists in the country, we were asked to come and help secure every other at-risk march that summer. Meanwhile, the public TV was running an aggressive campaign leading to the autumn elections. This time, the ruling party was planning on winning by inflaming homophobia in the country.

Spoiler alert: they won.

One evening I'm close to tears, and my roommate whispers: "Remember why you're doing this."

"And why am I doing this?" I ask. I'm drained, I'm exhausted, and others have to remind me of my own dreams.

"The children. The children see you being out and proud, they see you fight for yourself, they see you fight for them. They need to see."

She's right, but that night I was too bitter to admit it. When I was a teenager, Poland elected her first—and so far, only—transgender member of parliament. On TV, I saw a real, Polish, adult transgender woman being successful and professional. Those who grew up without anyone like them to look up to already know what I felt. I saw a superhero.

Except my superhero was mercilessly made fun of by the public. Everyone felt entitled to comment on how she looked, how she dressed, how she spoke. She was bullied. Resigned after her first term. But she existed, and she fought, and that was huge.

Huge, but somehow still not enough. We needed more than one person. She needed not to be alone. We needed a crowd.

Imagine the weight of this: I spent at least four Saturdays standing in line with police officers, the only difference between us being that they were fully-riot-ready-armed and I was wearing a white T-shirt. I also had a bullhorn, as if that would help. On the second march, I tied my bandana (first packed into my first-aid bag in case of tear gas) around my head like a pirate, a childish attempt to feel more confident. Behind us—a pride march, mainly wide-eyed teenagers. In front of us—the opposing team, throwing eggs and stones and informing us, quite clearly, about how much they despise the lot of us. The police officers put on helmets, as if afraid of the flying eggs—behind them, my friend was once again chanting her new refrain of "Rub the eggs in your hair, it's a free conditioner!"

We were not scared; the reality would hit us later when we rode the bus home, trying to remember what everyday life was like, again.

An image from Płock is stuck in my head—a man looking me in the eye and informing me, very calmly, that if Hitler were alive, he "would have me burnt." Once home, in the safe corner of my bedroom, I thought of my great-aunts tortured in Ravensbrück[4] seventy-five years ago, and I cried myself to sleep.

At church, with all of that in my heart, no one knew. They must know, I thought, it had been broadcast all over Europe. The anti-LGBTQ riots in Poland were a big thing. And so, I sat in the back pews and tried to convince myself that Jesus was sitting with me, that if he could, he would stand with me at that police line, defending the people I cared for. Only that's something I couldn't say aloud. I imagined some of the local brethren joining in to throw those eggs and those stones at me.

My branch president wondered why I stopped attending church.

I turned twenty-five in August that summer. It wouldn't seem like a big deal, except it was. When I was a teenager, before I understood complex statistical data, intersectionality, and layered marginalization, I read a study done in the U.S.A. that compared the life expectancy of different groups. A white, middle-class, cis, and straight male? Expected to live for about eighty years. A transgender person? Most likely to die between twenty and twenty-five.

I now know that this statistic is drastically lowered by the number of murdered American transgender women of color. I happen to be a white European trans man. But I was fifteen, deeply depressed, and confused, and I convinced myself that I'd never live past my twenty-fifth birthday.

As it turns out, I lived. The future is now.

Every once in a while, I went to church to see if it was as lonely as I remember. Mostly it was. Some days, hope shone on me through the clouds.

One Sunday I sat in the back row in Relief Society, holding baby Sawyer, not fully aware of the discussion happening around me. Sawyer napped peacefully, making little faces as he dreamt, and I rocked him, humming.

"If I love you so much, little boy," I told him, "then how much must your mummy love you. How much must God love you, little one?"

He might have thought me silly. "Silly grown-up, don't you know these things? Are you only discovering them now?"

All he knew in his short life was to be loved and cherished. I wished he could stay like this forever.

I rocked him. "Your mummy will love you no matter what. And so will God. There's nothing for you to worry about."

It was Sawyer's mummy who blessed me that Sunday after the summer of riots and the outpouring of hate. My face and my voice and the faces of my friends were on public TV, all of us called deviants, suspected of sexualizing minors. Church was hard with people staring at me warningly. But Sawyer's mummy, with two small children holding on to her skirt, sat next to me and handed me the baby with pleading eyes. He was tiny and brand new, and she was as tired as a young mum could be.

She tried apologizing later and said she was so overwhelmed and just needed help and knew I loved children. A bittersweet feeling came over me. "You trust me with your child. You don't think I'm a monster. You trust me to give loving care to a baby and it would never cross your mind that because I am queer, I would hurt him in any way."

As we talked, she was nursing him in the car, again showing the trust not many would extend to me. I can see in her eyes that she doesn't understand; she never realized that people can see something perverse behind my honest love for children.

You see, kindness comes in different ways.

Years ago, when I still thought I'd never come out and I was all out of hope, I shared my secret identity with a Relief Society sister as I helped her in her house. She listened, and she cried, and she hugged me. A few days later, she sent me an email, a thoughtful message that sparked a little bit of the lost hope in my soul.

"I don't know all the answers, but I know that God made you just as you are, and He understands your struggle. You are not bad, wrong, or evil.

"When your body is resurrected, I believe things will feel right. I have no idea what gender you will be, but I do believe everything will match, and you will have joy in your body and even in your gender. I suppose that may seem odd, but I really believe that."

NOTES

1. "Blessed are the peacemakers, for they will be called children of God" (NIV).
2. A honorific title awarded by the State of Israel to non-Jews who provided help to Jews during World War II as they faced extermination by the Nazi German authorities.
3. Third-hour refers to the third hour of LDS Church, which, until January, 2019 was when women and men met separately for Relief Society and Priesthood. In special circumstances, a combined meeting might be called during the third hour, which men and women would attend together. In January, 2019, the church moved to a two-hour block of meetings.
4. A Nazi concentration camp for female prisoners, operating in northern Germany between 1939 and 1945; one of the places where the Nazis conducted medical experiments on inmates without their consent.

31

With a Firm Hope

Miranda Ybarra

The morning my life changed started out as one of the best mornings of my life. It was Conference, we were with a recent convert and her husband. These people were like family to me and my companion. We even called them "Mom" and "Dad."

"Mi Hermanita" (as I lovingly called my companion) and I were sitting on the floor together, with me running my hands through the extra-plush mahogany rug. We had spent the morning with them, my companion had napped on their couch while "Mom" helped me French braid my hair and "Dad" made us the nicest breakfast we had as missionaries.

The warm spirit of the morning had left me when Elder Oaks took the podium.

He was decrying "cohabitation before marriage and same-sex relationships" from the podium. I had known I was pansexual all my life, but had decided to stay in the closet because I wanted to be a good church member. My hands curled into the carpet as an anchor to hold me in the moment.

As soon as the talk was over, I released a loud sigh that I hadn't realized I'd been holding in. The choir was singing now and "Dad" had gotten up to take our plates back to the kitchen. As he walked back, he and his wife said something that would permanently alter my life.

"It's so good he said all of those things. Same-sex support is really getting out of hand in the church. It's honestly gross to see."

"I agree, we have the Family Proclamation that expressly says to support traditional family values," his wife chimed in.

I couldn't focus for the rest of Conference. I found myself at their dining-room table, barely managing my anxiety by coloring in the pages they had printed for us. I grew up in the Pacific Northwest, and while I knew many people at home shared these same thoughts, it just wasn't talked about. I had expected their words from people on the street, or even random members. What I had not expected was those words to come from people I considered family.

When we got back to our apartment after Saturday morning session, I couldn't shake the feeling that had permeated me to my very core. People I loved wouldn't love me if they really knew me for who I was. I got back to our room and collapsed on the floor in tears.

"What's wrong, hermana?" My companion sat down next to me.

I knew I couldn't tell her. What if she told on me and I got sent home? I wasn't risking that.

"Leave me alone, I'll be fine, I just need to cry it out," I said and so I did. I sat on the floor in our apartment for hours, crying like the world was ending, which to me, it seemed like it was. With my eyes burning and my red splotchy face I determined that I was going to stop being pansexual. That was in the past.

And every day between that ten-second passing conversation between my "parents" and when I arrived home from my mission, I prayed and pleaded that I would magically wake up straight. That I would never have to worry about being queer again. But as I got home, I soon realized that things like that can't just be changed through prayer.

Little did I know that within six months of being home from my mission that I would finally make a queer friend. Trevor was a bisexual trans man living three thousand miles away from me. But also, the only person I could talk with about gay things.

I only knew him for three months when I felt that familiar twirl in my heart of a crush. I panicked, knowing that I could get in serious trouble for being with someone outside of the traditional gender roles in the church.

I took those feelings to the only place I knew to take them, the temple. I spent the whole time I was there thinking about Trevor. I tried to focus on the rituals taking place but my mind kept drifting back to the boy in New York. I left the celestial room with a strange sense of peace that it was the last time I'd be in there.

A month later, I found myself in JFK Airport after a red-eye flight that bridged those three thousand miles. I was exhausted and looking for someone I had only ever seen on a phone screen before. And when my eyes landed on him, after what felt like forever of waiting, my excited soul went still in its shell.

When I finally hugged him, I felt like I could actually understand the things people talked about in church. You know, all the nonsense about having agreed to find each other while we were in the premortal life. Being with him felt right. The whole trip I felt like I was just waiting for something to happen, for one of us to burst into flames or maybe feel an uncomfortable spirit at all. It never happened. All I felt was safe, happy, and loved.

The last night of my trip we lay in bed, joking, kissing, and talking about everything we could. When suddenly he sat up.

"I think, I think the Book of Mormon is true," he said suddenly. "I read Alma and just found so many answers that I've been looking for all my life, and I was wondering if you wanted to try going to church when we got to Washington."

But, we're queer. It won't go well for us. My mind was racing through all the possibilities: sure there were several bad outcomes, but there were also just as many good outcomes. We'd have to hold on to hope and take the chance. There was one thing I knew I wanted more than nearly anything, and it was to have my stereotypical Mormon life with the person I loved.

Four days after I left NYC, Trevor moved in with me and my family, and eight days after that, I came out publicly on the Saturday night before we went to church the first time as a couple. I went to bed, my heart racing, terrified that I would wake up to a host of angry messages. What I did wake up to was love from places I never would have expected.

At church that day, I bore my testimony that God loves everyone, gay or straight, and I felt so ready to take on the world. Until after sacrament, when I noticed that I had messages from that same family from my mission. They didn't tell me I was gross, but they did spout the same messages queer people become so familiar with, "it's just a trial," "things will be different in the next life," and, my personal least favorite, "all God asks of us is to keep the commandments, same for you as it is for me."

It has never been the same for you as it is for me.

After returning from church, Trevor got our pride flags from the walls, we turned up a pride playlist and we danced around our little room until we could feel the pride in who we were radiating from our skin.

Shortly after that, the bishop asked to meet with me at least once a week. Sometimes on Wednesdays, and sometimes on Sundays after church, but all meetings for the next two months boiled down to one topic: Why I wasn't "following the commandments," and why I should be.

The day after my twenty-second birthday in April, I got a letter inviting me to attend my disciplinary council to testify why I shouldn't be excommunicated from the church I had served a mission for less than a year earlier. The date of the council was just around three days after they gave me the letter. And so I showed up to defend to four straight, white, cis men that I should be just as allowed to love and date my partner as anyone else in the church.

"As it said in your letter, you are here because there is reason to believe that you have participated in conduct unbecoming a member of the church, including breaking the law of chastity. What do you have to say about this, Sister Ybarra?" The first counsellor read from a paper; the church letterhead was visible from across the room. I looked at these men that had been such supports to me in other contexts; now we all found ourselves in this office that was completely devoid of the Spirit.

I started to speak a defense I had typed into the Notes app of my phone in the days prior. My hands and voice both started shaking as I read the testimony of my love.

"You can try telling me that I just need faith and I can lead a happy life as a single sister, but you know what I have to say to that? I say shame on you. I sat every day on my mission trying not to hate myself. I prayed for God to take this away from me. I sat in members' homes, people who I loved unconditionally, and listened to them say I was gross, disgusting, and unnatural. In Mosiah 18, we read that Christ asks us to mourn with those that mourn. And not one person has even said a single apology for how I feel completely separated from the church I love."

Taking a deep breath, I looked in the eyes of my bishop before I continued.

I went on to testify about how I knew things would work out, if not in this life than in the next. I felt a confirmation that I was speaking the truth.

I walked out of the room, so my partner could share a testimony in my favor as well.

It ended up being a barrage of inappropriate questions about his gender, sexuality, and what exactly was in his pants.

Afterward, the leaders talked amongst themselves and we took selfies in the church hallway to avoid facing the impending feeling of panic.

"We have decided to restrict your membership privileges, you're disfellowshipped for the next six months. You can regain full membership if you end your relationship with Trevor, as well as meet with a LDS Family Services therapist and bishop for the next six months."

In plain speech, you can rejoin the church as a full member if you kick out the person you love, and go to conversion therapy.

My world was crushed. I was supposed to be Miranda the Mormon and that was pulled right out from underneath my feet. My entire world view was askew.

The next morning, I woke up preparing to go to work. About two hours before leaving, a thought entered my brain, "Let's find out if this *everything will be fixed in the afterlife* theory of theirs is correct." I knew this was serious because instead of falling into a frenzy, I calmly came up with a plan, and a backup plan.

Trevor noticed I was acting a little funny and sat me down to ask me how I was feeling. Thirty minutes later my partner admitted me into the psych ward. He spent the night, holding me, and listening to me cry about how I was sure that I was damning him, and how if he really wanted to join the church he should probably break up with me.

The next morning, I watched the sun rise out of the back of an ambulance as I was transported to the live-in facility. It took seven full days of therapy and being watched over until I felt like I wasn't ready to test this theory.

During that time, Trevor had his baptismal interview with the mission president to see if he could even join the church. It turned into a nightmarish scene with the mission president yelling at him that he couldn't love God and be trans.

Less than six months later, I took my name off of the records of the church, with the hope that should things get better I could come back easier than if I had been excommunicated. I feel this hope like a seed within me. Every day I meet more members, missionaries, and leaders who are willing to love and accept us for who we are.

And so it is with a firm hope that we look towards the future, a future where we can be ourselves and loved, a future where we can serve in our wards, and a future where we can be sealed together.

Firm, steadfast, immovable.

Hope.

Minha Auto Aceitação
(My Self-Acceptance)

Cristina Moraes
Translated by the Author

32

Nascida de bons pais, vivi uma infância feliz. Sem contatos com nada que não fosse belo e cheio de sonhos. Mas tudo se transformou no início da minha adolescência. Grande foi o meu choque ao observar minha mente percorrer sentimentos que eu nem sabia o que era.

Minha mente me mostrava a imagem de um corpo feminino, e isso me assustou e me diminuiu grandemente.

Fui criada por um método rigoroso, não nos era permitido pensar em qualquer coisa que não fosse estritamente religioso. Eu não sabia o que era esse desejo, eu só entendia que não era permitido. A minha adolescência foi suprimida. Eu tinha medo de pensar em uma mulher. Por isso eu estudava muito e me dedicava a tudo que fosse considerado louvável e de acordo ao padrão divino.

Meu medo era tão grande que as vezes eu parava de respirar por medo que meus pensamentos fossem revelados. Eu não suportei essa pressão, ainda na adolescência aproximei-me de pessoas que eu presumia que tinham os mesmos desejos que eu, mas nunca tive qualquer contato físico ou amoroso com nenhuma mulher. Era sempre apenas uma aproximação para entender quem eram e o que eu era.

Nesse momento o meu sofrimento começou. Fui drasticamente criticada e ferida em minha alma, pois minha família jamais iria permitir isso. Eu fui severamente machucada fisicamente e castigada por minha mãe. E minha alma estava destroçada, eu tinha medo de Deus e me tornei uma pessoa triste.

Eu ouvi naquela época a primeira condenação. Ouvi minha mãe dizer: "Se você continuar pensando em ficar com uma mulher, você será expulsa de casa". Eu nunca tentei tirar a minha vida, mas desejei que Deus fizesse isso milagrosamente. Eu queria deixar de sofrer!

Eu perdi as contas de quantas vezes fui agredida ou castigada por pensar em "estár com uma mulher". Fui deixada com fome; nenhum alimento me foi oferecido por dias. Minha mãe fazia isso como forma de me trazer a cura, com o objetivo de que eu deixasse esses pensamentos fora da minha cabeça. Mas Deus me ajudou a continuar amando minha mãe. Ela não entendia. Na verdade, nem eu entendia. Ela só agia porque pensava que era possível curar minha mente e corpo. Eu perguntava a Deus: Senhor, o que é isso? Por que sou diferente? Eu não queria ser diferente.

A Igreja de Jesus Cristo dos Santos dos Últimos Dias foi como um milagre emergencial. Eu esperava me fechar e encontrar resignação divina. Eu vivi 100% dedicada às coisas da igreja. Servi posteriormente uma missão, trabalhei todos os dias da minha vida para suprir e tirar aquele desejo da minha alma.

Pensei que tudo tinha passado depois de tantos anos. Mas nada mudou. Eu ainda sentia a mesma dor e falta de explicação. Eu dormia chorando e acordava ainda pior. Eu queria que Deus falasse comigo e me ajudasse a me curar de uma doença.

Muito depois da missão pela igreja, eu conheci e tive o primeiro contato com uma mulher de forma física, e aquilo foi algo libertador, maravilhoso, e ao mesmo tempo sufocante e triste.

Vivi uma vida dupla. Eu queria manter minha vida na igreja e ao mesmo tempo um relacionamento. Isso não era possível. Eu escolhi a igreja. Mas eu era uma capa de felicidade externa e uma tristeza interna.

Quando conheci a minha esposa Viviane Moraes eu via nela toda a doçura que eu precisava. Eu entendia o verdadeiro amor. Foi nessa época que o Pai finalmente falou comigo e eu passei a saber que Ele me amava como eu era.

Passei a viver, e comecei a sentir felicidade. Ainda não me aceitava verdadeiramente, mas eu já conseguia viver.

Em 2015, eu conheci a Afirmação.

A Afirmação causou em meu coração o efeito que o próprio nome sugere "Afirmação". Ao conhecer a Afirmação e começar a trabalhar nessa obra, surgiu uma certeza de ser feliz sendo um Mórmon LGBTQ.

Hoje reconheço que a minha condição sexual não me torna uma pessoa menor que as demais. Tenho certeza do amor do Pai Celestial por mim e todos os meus amigos GLBT.

Ao receber o conforto da Afirmação, a minha forma de ver o mundo mudou, e hoje possuo total respeito por minha própria pessoa.

A Afirmação provou um milagre transformador dentro de minha alma. Ajudou-me a ouvir a voz do Pai Celestial dizendo: "Estarei sempre de mãos dadas contigo minha filha". A sensação de poder saber que não sou uma filha deixada de lado por causa da minha condição sexual é muito boa.

Ao receber o milagre transformador em minha vida, passei a buscar que outros também recebessem essa transformação. Sou extremamente grata por fazer parte dessa obra no Brasil. Servir como Presidente da Afirmação no Brasil é algo fantástico. As pessoas ansiavam por uma voz, um conforto, um ombro amigo.

Todos possuem o direito de saber que são filhos especiais de nosso Pai Celestial. Não importa sua condição sexual, o que conta é o coração. O coração precisa ser bom.

Aprendi com a Afirmação de que não precisamos ser aceitos, precisamos de respeito. Respeito a nossa condição, respeito-a como pessoa e cidadão.

Hoje eu possuo a verdadeira auto aceitação. Eu entendo o meu lugar e o propósito da minha vida. Eu me aceito e sou extremamente feliz em ser uma mulher lésbica. Eu sei que sou uma filha especial de nosso Pai Celestial. Que o amor dele é total por mim e todos os LGBTQ. Tenho um casamento abençoado com a minha esposa há 14 anos. Percebo as bençoes divinas em nosso casamento. Eu sou muito feliz.

Sou Cristina Moraes. Sou Brasileira, pós-Graduada em Administração e Engenharia da Qualidade, casada com uma linda esposa e uma mulher muito feliz por ter superado as minhas dores. Possuo sim uma herança Mórmon e acredito que o Senhor ainda revelará milagres em nossas vidas.

Born to goodly parents, I lived a happy childhood, filled with only that which was beautiful and full of dreams. But everything changed in my early teens. Great was my shock as I saw my mind process feelings, feelings that I didn't understand and couldn't explain.

My mind showed me the image of a female body, and it scared me and greatly diminished me.

I was raised rigidly. We were not allowed to think of anything that wasn't strictly religious. I didn't know what this desire was—I just understood it wasn't allowed. My teenage years were suppressed. I was afraid to think of a woman. That is why I studied hard and dedicated myself to everything that was considered praiseworthy and in accordance with the divine standard.

My fear was so great that sometimes I stopped breathing for fear that my thoughts would be revealed. I could not stand this pressure, yet as a teenager I approached people I assumed had the same desires as me, but I never had any physical or romantic contact with any woman. Just remained close to understand who they were and what I was.

In this time, my suffering began. I was sharply criticized and wounded in my soul because my family would never allow it. I was severely physically injured and punished by my mother. And my soul was broken, I was afraid of God, and I became a sad person.

I heard my mother say, "If you keep thinking of staying with a woman, you will be thrown out of the house." I never tried to take my life, but wished for a miracle that God would take it for me. I wanted to stop suffering!

I lost count of how many times I was beaten or punished for thinking of "being with a woman." I was left hungry—no food was offered to me for days. My mother did this as a way of curing me, so that I would leave these thoughts out of my head. But God helped me to continue loving my mother, though she didn't understand. In fact, I didn't even understand. She only acted that way because she thought it was possible to cure my mind and body.

I asked God, *Lord, what is this? Why am I different? I didn't want to be different.*

The Church of Jesus Christ of Latter-day Saints was like a much-needed miracle. I lived 100% completely dedicated to everything to do with the church. Serving a mission afterwards, I worked every day of my life to suppress and remove that desire from my soul.

I thought it was all over with after so many years. But nothing changed, I still felt the same pain and lack of explanation.

I would cry myself to sleep and wake up even worse. I wanted God to talk to me and help me be cured from an illness.

Long after the LDS Church mission, I met and had my first physical contact with a woman, and that was liberating, wonderful, and at the same time suffocating and sad.

I lived a double life, I wanted to keep my life in church and at the same time have a relationship. This was not possible. I chose the church. But I was wearing a mask of outer happiness with an inner sadness.

That's when I met my wife Viviane Moraes. I saw in her all the sweetness that I needed. I understood true love. It was at this time that Father finally spoke to me and I came to know that He loved me as I was.

I started to live, started to feel happiness. I still didn't truly accept myself, but I could at least manage to live.

In 2015, I met Affirmation.[1]

Affirmation caused in my heart the effect that their very name suggests, "affirmation." As I got to know the organization and started to get involved in this work, a certainty arose of being happy being an LGBTQ Mormon.

Today I recognize that my sexual orientation does not make me a person smaller than others. I am sure of Heavenly Father's love for me and for all my LGBTQ friends.

Receiving the comfort of Affirmation has changed my view of the world. Today I have total respect for myself.

Affirmation caused a transformational miracle within my soul. It helped me hear Heavenly Father's voice saying, "I will always be with you, holding your hands, my daughter." The feeling of being able to know that I am not a daughter left to the side because of my sexual orientation is so good.

As I received the transformative miracle in my life, I began to seek others to receive this transformation as well. I am extremely grateful to be part of this work in Brazil. Serving as President of Affirmation in Brazil is fantastic. People longed for a voice, a comfort, a work, a friend.

Everyone has the right to know that they are special children of our Heavenly Father. No matter your sexual orientation, what counts is the heart. The heart needs to be good.

I learned from the statement that we don't need to be accepted— we need respect. Respect our orientation, respect as a person, and citizen.

Today I have true self-acceptance. I understand my place and the purpose of my life. I accept myself and I am extremely happy to be a lesbian woman. I know that I am a special daughter of our Heavenly Father. His love is total for me and for all LGBTQ. I have had a blessed marriage with my wife for 14 years. I realize the divine blessings in our marriage. I'm very happy.

I am Cristina Moraes, I am Brazilian, postgraduate in administration and quality engineering, married with a beautiful wife, and a woman who is very happy to have overcome my pain.

I do have a Mormon heritage, and I believe the Lord will still reveal miracles in our lives.

NOTE

1. Affirmation (affirmation.org) is a support group for LGBTQ Mormons, their families, and friends. Like the Mormon Church, it has a global presence.

33

E Se? (What If?)

Irving Diego Santos
Translated by the Author

Oi, o meu nome é Irving. Tenho vinte e quatro anos e sou um homem trans Mórmon. Quando eu soube desse projeto, quis muito escrever, não só para contar a minha história, mas também para conseguir uma ligação com alguém que entendesse onde a minha religião se encaixa em tudo isso.

Espero que eu possa ajudar.

Quando eu tinha dois anos, minha mãe recebeu duas sisteres em nossa casa e decidiu ouvir a mensagem delas. Desde então ela nunca parou de ir à igreja e sempre me levava com ela, até o momento em que percebi, quando eu tinha treze anos, que eu gostava de garotas. A princípio eu achei que era apenas isso, uma garota que gostava de garotas, então continuei indo à igreja normalmente, porque eu nunca achei que isso fosse algo errado. Para mim ... sempre foi amor, e amor não é algo errado. Digo, o Senhor não quer que você quebre a lei da castidade, claro, mas não que você seja uma pessoa que não ama. Então continuei indo à igreja normalmente, até os meus quatorze a quinze anos, quando comecei a faltar a reunião sacramental aos domingos e a frequentar apenas o seminário e outras atividades. Eu ainda podia disfarçar bem, mas comecei a gostar de uma garota de dentro da igreja, uma amiga de quem eu era muito próximo.

Ela era asiática-brasileira, usava as roupas mais legais, e ouvia as músicas mais legais, e desde a primeira vez que eu a vi na igreja eu pensei "Wow, eu preciso me aproximar dessa garota". Mas até então eu só achava que ela era muito legal mesmo, o sentimento e interesse se desenvolveu depois quando consegui me aproximar dela. Ficamos amigos e eu pude notar que além de incrível por fora, ela era incrível por dentro também. Eu nunca contei para ela sobre os meus sentimentos. Até hoje ela não sabe, pois me afastei da igreja e deixei de ir antes de contar.

Eu pensei que eu era uma garota lésbica até perceber que eu era diferente das minhas outras amigas lésbicas. Notei que eu era a única pessoa que queria nascer homem cis, que não estava contente com o meu corpo quando elas eram felizes assim. Após de pesquisar muito, ler muitos depoimentos, ponderar sobre o assunto e muitas vezes até fugir dele, eu me assumi homem trans aos 17 anos, e toda a minha vida e infância passou a fazer sentido. Quando parei de fugir dessa descoberta e finalmente me aceitei, um novo mundo se abriu. Foi a primeira vez que o verde ficou mais verde, o vermelho ficou mais vermelho, e eu realmente soube que era possível me sentir tão confortável, transparente, e, acima de tudo, fiel à minha criança interior que sempre quis isso. Então o meu próximo passo foi me ajoelhar e conversar com o Senhor. Pedi que ele me desse um sinal ou que confortasse meu coração, que ele me abençoasse e me desse forças pra enfrentar tudo que eu passaria a enfrentar a partir daquele momento. Desde aquela conversa que tive com Ele, eu percebi que Ele nunca errou em me fazer dessa forma. Eu entendi pessoalmente porque vim assim e o agradeci por isso. Assim me senti mais leve ainda e livre para ser quem eu era.

A segunda vez que o verde ficou mais verde e o vermelho mais vermelho foi quando juntei a outra metade do meu quebra-cabeça, que foi o momento em que notei todos os sinais da minha vida dentro da igreja. Lembro-me de que não usava saias e vestidos até ser batizado, nunca gostei, nunca me senti à vontade na Organização das Moças, nunca me importou onde elas compravam aquele vestido, aquelas saias, mesmo que eu achasse que as roupas eram bonitas, era como se eu estivesse fantasiado, não confortável. Sempre senti mais interesse nos ternos bem cortados e feitos sob medida, nas gravatas, nos sapatos. Às vezes até perguntava onde eles tinham encontrado aquela gravata legal. Me lembro também da sensação de ver meninos mais novos que eu fazendo treze anos e começando a entregar o sacramento, meninos um pouco mais velhos abençoando o sacramento, homens batizando pessoas, confirmando e, principalmente, a coisa que eu mais quis: servindo uma missão. Durante meus pensamentos, voltei a lembrar daquela garota, aquela minha amiga que eu me interessei quando éramos amigos e eu ainda ia a igreja. Notei que se eu tivesse vindo ao mundo como homem cis, baseado em como gostávamos de ser amigos, e baseado na nossa faixa etária, provavelmente teríamos tido algo. E ... quem sabe não mais do que aquilo? Até hoje isso vem a minha mente de vez em quando, o "e se?"

O ponto é que os meus amigos me entendem, sempre me apoiaram, e entendem toda essa questão. Tenho alguns amigos trans na cidade com que eu posso dividir minhas experiências pessoais sobre ser trans e tudo sobre isso.Mas eles nunca vão entender como é dentro da religião, nem a vontade de ter um sacerdócio, um chamado, e estar firme na igreja. Eu nunca dividi esse sentimento com outro homem trans Mórmon.Eu me sinto muito solitário nessa parte da minha vida é triste não poder soltar isso para alguém que diga "Sim, eu também vêm me senti assim."

Felizmente nunca sofri muita transfobia na minha vida. A minha mãe por mais que não goste não me impede de viver como gosto, não solta palavras de ódio, não me expulsou da casa, não me bateu, nem nada de ruim que costuma acontecer com pessoas LGBTQ. O resto da minha família sempre tenta se adaptar às mudanças e também nunca tentou me machucar de nenhuma forma. Além de algumas pessoas da igreja que sempre vêm aqui e ainda me chamam pelo nome antigo (mesmo que eu já tenha mudado nos meus documentos oficiais), consigo viver uma vida passável na rua e empregos. Sou muito grato por isso, por tantos privilégios.

Espero que a minha história tenha ajudado no projeto de alguma forma. Eu sei que não foi uma história específica como procuravam, mas eu agradeço a oportunidade de contá-la.

Hi, my name is Irving. I am twenty-four years old and I'm a trans Mormon man. When I heard about the project, I really wanted to write, not only to tell my story, but also to get a connection with someone who understood where my religion fits in with it.

I hope I can help.

When I was two years old, my mother received two sister missionaries in our house and decided to hear their message. Since then, she never stopped going to church and always took me with her until the moment that I noticed, when I was thirteen years old, that I liked girls. At first, I thought it was just that: a girl who liked girls. I kept going to church like normal, because I never thought that it was wrong. For me ... it has always been love, and love is not something that is wrong. I mean, the Lord does not want you to break the law of chastity, of course, but it doesn't mean that you're a person who doesn't love. So, I kept going to church until I was about fourteen or fifteen years old. I started to miss sacrament meeting on Sundays and only attended seminary and other church activities. I could still disguise well, but I started to like a girl from in the church, a friend to whom I was very close.

She was an Asian-Brazilian girl, and she had the coolest clothes, listened to the coolest songs, and since the first time I saw her at church, I thought, "Wow, I need to get closer to this girl." But up until then, I only thought she was really nice—the feeling and interest developed later. When I got closer to her, we became friends and I noticed that besides being amazing on the outside, she was amazing on the inside, too. I never told her about my feelings. To this day she doesn't know, because I walked away from the church and let go before telling.

I thought I was a lesbian girl until I realized that I was different from my other friends who were lesbians. I noticed that I was the only one who wanted to be born cis man, who wasn't content with my body when they were happy with theirs. After much research, reading many testimonials, pondering the subject and often even running away from it, at seventeen I became a trans man. After that, my whole life and childhood made sense. When I stopped running away from that discovery and finally accepted myself, a new world opened. It was the first time that green seemed more green, red seemed more red. I really didn't know it was possible to feel so comfortable, so transparent and, most of all, faithful to my inner child who had always wanted it. So, my next step was to kneel and talk to the Lord, to ask him to give me a sign or to comfort my heart, to bless me, and to give me the strength to face all that I would face from that moment on. Since that conversation that I had with Him, I realized that He never made a mistake in making me that way, I personally understood why I came this way and thanked Him for it. I felt even lighter and free to be who I was.

The second time the green seemed greener and the red redder was when I put the other half of my puzzle together. It was the moment that I noticed all of the signs from my life inside the church. I remembered that I didn't wear skirts and dresses until I was baptized, I never liked it. I never felt comfortable in the Young Women's Organization. I never cared where they bought that dress, that skirt, even if I thought the clothes were pretty. It was as if I was always in a costume, but never comfortable. I was always more interested in the well-cut and tailored suits, ties, shoes, sometimes even wondering where they had found their cool tie. I also remember the feeling of seeing younger boys than me turning thirteen and starting to pass the sacrament, slightly older boys blessing the sacrament, men baptizing people, confirming them. What I wanted most of all was to serve a mission like the other guys. While I was thinking, I remembered that girl, that friend of mine I was interested in when I was still going to church. I remember thinking that maybe if I had come into the world as a cis man, based on how we liked being friends and based on our own age group, we probably would have had something and . . . who knows what could have happened? To this day it comes to my mind from time to time. What if?

The point is that my friends understand me, always support me and understand this whole question. I have some trans friends in town that I can share my personal experiences with about being trans. But they will never understand what it's like with religion. They will never understand what it's like to want to have the priesthood, a calling, and to be firm in the church. I have never shared this feeling with another trans Mormon man and I feel very lonely in this part of my life. It's sad not being able to tell anyone who can say, "Yes, I felt that way, too."

Fortunately, I have never suffered from very much transphobia in my life. My mother, however much she dislikes it, does not prevent me from living as I please. She does not say hateful things, didn't expel me from home, didn't beat me, or anything bad that usually happens to LGBTQ people. The rest of my family always tries to adapt to the changes and never tried to hurt me in any way. Except for some people from the church who always come here and still call me by my old name (even though I've already changed it in my official documents), I can live a passable life on the street and at work. I am really grateful for that, because compared to others, I have so many privileges that they sometimes do not.

I hope my story helped in the project in some way. It may not have been the specific story you were looking for, but I appreciate the opportunity to tell it.

Seeking Courage, Pride, and Limits

34

Chelsea Gibbs

For about a week in eleventh grade, I made a habit of visiting the last stall in the bathroom by my math class. This wasn't for OCD or bladder-related reasons. It was because next to the ongoing "hot guys!" list in that stall, someone had started one for "hot girls" in our school. I was mesmerized by this list. Was it a joke? Were the girls who started it gay, or was it written in an admiring, no-homo kind of way? A number of names sprang to mind that I wanted to add, but what if somebody somehow recognized my handwriting and said I was gay?

Still I returned to the list every day not only to see whose names were added, but to feel a little less alone. There were other girls noticing the other girls at school, maybe in a gay way. I resolved to add the name of a cute girl myself, armed with a Sharpie and planning to write with my left hand to help disguise my handwriting.

I ran to the stall before math. My heart sank. Next to the list, three different handwritings had added the following in big, block letters: "EWWW," "GROSS," and "FUCKING DYKES." The Sharpie stayed in my backpack and when I braved visiting the stall again days later, all the graffiti had been washed off. The "hot guys" list eventually returned, but the "hot girls" list never did.

During my first semester as a grad student at USC, I began developing feelings for a girl, feelings which barreled past the dismissible crushes I'd had over the years and head-on into love. Let's call her Taylor. She and I had never met face-to-face; we actually became friends through the website Tumblr as outspoken, self-professed straight fans of a TV show with a predominantly lesbian fanbase. We were knee-deep in fandom activity, sharing our own queer theories and fan works. The novelty of having two straight women be so prominent in such a gay fandom was pointed out to us, and we began exchanging private messages. This ultimately turned into swapping our numbers so we could text each other outside the safe anonymity of Tumblr, and suddenly I became one of those people who couldn't stand to be separated from her phone—Taylor would text me at all hours of the day and I didn't want to miss a single message. How could I help myself, when she would send me hilarious observations on a mundane day, or make my heart stop with sudden comments like, "I wish you were here." We'd been talking a lot about our shared love of rainy weather, an unfortunate affection as we both lived in very dry places, so I asked, "Why? Is it raining there?" Her response was, "No. I just wish you were here." I did, too, more and more.

Like me, Taylor had been raised a devout Christian, and we talked in depth about faith and other personal matters, all the while still using our Tumblr pseudonyms and not exchanging pictures to retain a sense of distance and safety from our online queer dabbling. We started using pet names and went overboard on heart emojis in private, as a joke at first, but soon those became sincere. In time, I realized I was starting to fall for her, as I wanted to learn everything about her and tell her things I'd never told anyone else. Well, almost everything: the closest we came to acknowledging that our friendship might have shifted into attraction was a text she sent me out of the blue that asked: "Do we ever confuse you?" We didn't, but I wasn't brave enough to tell her that yet. I remember sitting in my parents' living room, staring at that text, both dying to know what specifically had prompted her to ask me this and feeling a prick of concern over the potential ramifications of my reply. I chickened out and said something like "Sometimes," and when she didn't respond right away, I made a joke to change the subject.

Unlike my uber-closeted undergrad experience at BYU, I was surrounded by out, happy, queer classmates at USC. Still I was afraid to ask them for advice in regard to Taylor, because talking about the attraction would make it real and I wasn't ready for that. What was my great catalyst to coming out? A damn Disney movie. Elsa's mantra of "conceal, don't feel" and "be the good girl you always have to be" in *Frozen* jumped out at me as I sat in the theater, transfixed. I will never forget the strength "Let It Go" gave me when I first experienced it, like someone casting a rope out to save me from my own "kingdom of isolation." Here was a character casting off decades of shame, finding joy in the unique power she had been given and told to fear. The movie left me yearning for a taste of that happiness, and I knew I would never get it if I continued to conceal my feelings.

I went back home for the winter holiday a couple weeks later. At midnight on New Year's Eve, under the covers in bed, I texted Taylor to tell her how I felt. She was with family and couldn't talk. The next day she agreed to call me, but I, too, was wary of being overheard by family. I drove to another part of town to talk in privacy and got restless sitting in the car. It was twelve degrees outside and snow was on the ground, but I went out to walk in it while I talked to Taylor. Even with gloves and boots on, I felt my extremities starting to go numb as we cried on the phone together, wading through the perils of internalized homophobia.

At first, I was feeling pretty good about my ability to assuage her anxieties as they cropped up, like hitting pitches sent down the middle of the plate. We still hadn't actually exchanged pictures at this point, and she insisted she was too ordinary looking for me to really have a crush on. I almost laughed as I assured her that looks didn't matter because I'd fallen for who she was as a person. She didn't understand the point of theorizing about a relationship when we lived a couple of states away from each other, and I told her that long drives were a breeze for me.

Soon, though, there came a pivot that I couldn't deflect. In a tone of utter disbelief, she asked, "Your family would be okay with this?" I remember the shock in her voice—tinged with what sounded like contempt—when I almost guiltily explained that I had a brother who was gay and had been out for a while, which had given me the security blanket of knowing my family wouldn't turn me out. Taylor did not have that luxury. She was normally very well-spoken, but here she was tripping over her words for once and my memory of her further reasoning comes out in short bursts: "My family would never—I can't even imagine a world where they would be okay with—could never go on a date with a girl—they wouldn't accept—"

We didn't resolve anything, despite talking for well over an hour. We just cried and got more confused. When I got back home, I was shaking so hard from the cold that I couldn't speak without stuttering. I couldn't give my family a good explanation for why I'd been out in the snow for so long. I was "the good kid"; despite my parents' long, rocky journey to become LGBTQ allies, I'd still assigned myself the task of being their one child who *was* a good Mormon, which meant following the church's tenets, which meant I couldn't like girls. I wasn't ready for them to know about Taylor. They didn't press me about my walk. My mom just started drawing a warm bath for me while my brother piled warm blankets on me. I could barely interact with him because my mind was buzzing with Taylor's vocalized fears, and my heart was aching over the love she was frightened of losing from the devout family who meant everything to her.

Though we eventually met in person and had some long-distance semi-relationship starts and stops, in time it fell apart when Taylor concluded that "same-sex attraction" was unacceptable to God and therefore unacceptable to her. I got the impression that the online space where we'd first met had given her a warped perspective of what it meant to be gay. While that insular world gave her her only window into the lives of mostly anti-religious queer women she couldn't relate to, I had finally found LGBTQ LDS meetings within driving distance (100 miles) and gotten great support there. I asked Taylor once if that might've made a difference for her, having an in-person support group of queer religious people. "Maybe" was all she said, and we never spoke of her orientation again. But as a good friend, she was open to hearing about my ongoing journey of queer Mormon womanhood.

That journey got its big boost the first time I went to the international Affirmation conference in September of 2015, and it was brimming with a joyous celebration of progress. The Supreme Court had just legalized same-sex marriage nationwide a couple months earlier, and everyone was riding this optimistic wave of change, seemingly inevitable even for the LDS Church. Brimming with nerves and excitement, I attended a break-out session for queer women and gender minorities. About ten of us met in a circle in a small room, people I'd been waiting my whole life to meet without even knowing it, and every stranger I shook hands with became an instant friend because we were all in this together. We nodded in sympathy together; we laughed loudly when sharing joyful experiences. The rainbow ceiling felt shattered and we didn't have to be quiet anymore: we could laugh and shout and cry all we wanted, which made our tiny gathering feel enormous. Everyone at the conference felt like pioneers whose time had come.

Less than two months after that jubilant event, the church's infamous now-retracted Exclusion Policy was leaked. I remember scrolling through Facebook and seeing headline after headline shared, unable to wrap my head around the fact that it could possibly be true. It was a devastating blow, and called to mind the crushing of hope I'd felt after seeing that list on my high-school restroom stall, the first indicator that there were girls who might think like me at my school, only to see their desires disparaged and erased. I think that pendulum swing really affected the attitude of Mormons who came out immediately before the policy was announced. Many of my friends abandoned the church or church-adjacent spaces at once, and I myself started feeling like a stranger in a strange land whenever I made it to church. Suddenly things I'd found familiar, even comforting, my whole life—the grandmotherly fabric of the pews, the burlap walls, the shape of the podium—felt inherently distancing. Hymns sounded like they were droned, not sung. The people sitting around me, who I'd been close to for years, seemed like another species. Their smiles and hugs and "how are you doing?"s were heartfelt, but I was numbed by the dissonance that came from their love joined with their unwavering devotion to the church. "This policy is awful," a well-meaning Relief Society leader confided to me in the privacy of the hallway with a genuinely sorrowful expression. "I don't agree with it," a primary teacher whispered to me as she embraced me. "What can we do?" another sister asked rhetorically, shrugging her shoulders.

What could they do? Rather than murmur about their sadness or guilt to me in secret, they could have used their voices to speak up, which is what I had learned to do. No more being cornered into silence by shame or fears.

Recently I was tracked down by some sister missionaries who had been dispatched to find out why I hadn't been coming to church. I was in the middle of doing some work, so I didn't have time to invite them in for a conversation. I got right down to the point: "Well, I'm gay." They honestly seemed less scandalized by this statement than the fact that I'd opened the door in a tank top. They were quick to assure me that the ward was very accepting, which I had no trouble believing. "That's very nice," I said sincerely. The sisters seemed surprised that this information didn't make me jump at the invitation to return to church. I explained, "The line is, 'The people aren't perfect, but the gospel is.' I've had the chance to meet a lot of really near-perfect people at church, who have been wholly accepting of my identity. But I don't fit in the gospel the church prescribes, unless I'm happy to squander decades in celibacy. That's not perfect to me." Awkward, but firm, and they didn't push it. They gave me a card with a picture of Jesus and their phone numbers written on it, in case I'd ever like to talk more.

"Can we leave you with a word of prayer?" they asked.

I sighed, ready to let them in to do so. Turning down a polite, harmless request felt rude, and I bore no ill will to these individual missionaries. But my reluctance gave me pause and I realized, *you don't have to let them in if you don't want to. You can talk with missionaries and other Mormons any time, but on* your *terms.* They'd asked, and it was my right to decline.

"No thanks, that's okay," I said. "I'm good."

And I am.

The Binary

Ari Glass

35

I want to start by saying I'm not out and proud. I mostly live in the quietness of the margins.

When people say the word *binary*, I think of zeros and ones. When people say church, especially on Sundays like today, I think of Relief Society and priesthood. I think of the relentless slicing forces of all the borders I see drawn around me and they threaten to cut me in two; I feel powerless. This is my story about how I'm not a one or a zero, a pink or a blue, an M or an F—I'm just me, a unique and valid child of a loving God.

The gender binary is ingrained in the church (as it is in the rest of society). When I was fifteen, I wanted to play cricket. The options I had were to play on Sundays on the women's team or on Saturdays on the boys' team. This was when I first fully realized that I didn't like being a girl. Don't get me wrong, there are great things about womanhood or whatever, but it just ... isn't for me.

I remember my first training with the boys' team.

"Hey boys, this is your new teammate, Ariana," said my half-Kiwi coach. I already wanted to hide. 1) Everyone was looking at me—I stuck out like a sore thumb. 2) "Ariana."

I'm *not* "Ariana," I'm *Ari*. It has always felt more like me—like my name. But now I would spend the entire season being "Ariana."

The awkward fourteen-year-old boys all looked at me blankly.

Training started with a net session, and I was a bowler. And really, all I wanted to be in that moment was a bowler. Not a female bowler, not the girl on the boy' team, just the bowler. I remember the way I would bowl so the ball floated through the air, spinning before changing course when it hit the ground, and I remember how I would have to try to readjust my bra after that without anyone noticing. *Why do I have to have breasts?* I've always hated them, but right then I hated them even more.

And to top it off, training finished with Coach yelling, "Good session boys and *girl*."

Great, I thought, *singled out as a girl again*. This was the first time I thought maybe I wasn't a girl.

For me, growing to accept being nonbinary has taken years because I grew up in a world where that term didn't exist. Australian media only ever showed the limited view of feminine, gay men.

I learnt what a bisexual was at fifteen while sitting in a French class that was way too hard for me. My friend was sitting next to me, and we were supposed to be watching a documentary about youth smoking in France, but all I wanted to know was what the term *bi* meant. My friend had used the term at lunch, and I was so confused. So, on a pink sticky note I wrote, "What does *bi* mean?"

Back came the useless reply, "Bisexual."

Oh no, I'm going to look like a homophobic fool, fitting all the Mormon stereotypes.

"What does *bisexual* mean?"

And in her messy but also somehow tidy handwriting came back the reply "I'm bisexual, it means I like both boys and girls."

That's when it hit me: didn't everyone?

I sweated through that French class filling that sticky note with questions to the backdrop of teenage smoking in France.

It wasn't until three years later that I use the label *bisexual* on myself. That year was also when I started to learn about being trans. I had a friend that I called "Das" because they weren't sure what gender they were and *Das* is the gender-neutral definitive in German. Now I am my own Das.

I remember the first time I wore a suit to church. It was summer, and it was Relief Society week. I sat on the end of the row of the blue stackable chairs by the door in a position that I thought would allow me the quickest escape even though I was always one of the first ones there. Sister Y was teaching that day, or, as I called her, Sister "Make-Everyone-Bi." I mean,

I was already bi—I've always been bi—but she was stunning and no one could *ever* know I thought that. There is this awkwardness of there only being two of us in the room. I know I'm never going to speak first. So, I'm sitting there in my suit—well, not really a suit: a mint green button down, red bow tie, and dark blue chinos—shaking like heck because I have restless legs and autism and anxiety. Somehow Sister Y cuts through all that and says to me "Sister Me, I love your bow tie."

I am completely thrown off guard. My mouth lets out a "I'm good" before realizing this was not the correct answer. Looking over the light blue curtains that surround us in our classroom on the stage, I note it is too early to leave. C'mon, think.

"Thanks, I bought it off eBay." Good save.

"I get all of my husband's ties on eBay," I manage to capture before I can't hear anything else over my anxiety and before long the class starts.

But later that night, I am thinking about "Sister, I love your bowtie." I don't understand how "sister," something for females, and "bowtie," something often associated with males, go in the same sentence. How can you say that you love that I'm pushing the gender binary and in that same breath push me into that binary?

Today is my first Relief Society Sunday in a new ward. Again, I'm wearing the mint green shirt, but this time with a floral bow tie—my style has evolved significantly, what can I say? I'm in Relief Society and all they know is the binary, therefore, I must be a girl. But boy, are they wrong. I've yet to test the waters of acceptance and tolerance in this new ward, so for now I'll continue living in my invisible identities.

For me being nonbinary fits with gospel doctrine but not church culture, but doctrinal analysis isn't part of my story.

I don't think God cares about our gender as a whole, but They care about it when it is important to us because They care about us. They care about us and if I am to believe in a loving God and a merciful God, then Their gospel will be for me, nonbinary and all. However, teachings of the church, of Dallin H. Oaks, often tell us that we as queer members are wrong and broken, but that is not the God I know. To summarize, being queer has challenged my testimony. Identifying as nonbinary means I'm free to not be a girl. I now use they/them pronouns with my family and I feel the most me I ever have.

Five Stories on Why I Don't Belong

Chris Davis

36

1980

My feet dangle inches from the carpeted floor. I silently wonder whether the white cinder-block walls and frosted windows are meant to hold things in or keep things out. The bishop is sitting across from me with his fingers knit together. His question hangs in the air between us. "Do you want to be baptized?"

I know what he wants me to say. My mother waits outside, anticipating my wholehearted agreement to join her church. This is something she has looked forward to since my parents' divorce. Even though I am only nine, I understand that there is a power struggle between my parents, and in so many ways, I am at the center of this tug-of-war. I recall the words my father told me to say in this moment, and I rehearse them to the bishop. "I'd like to wait until I'm sixteen, so I have more experience to make a better decision."

His eyebrows shoot up. This is not the customary response to his question. I have stumped the bishop and I think about how proud Dad would be to see me stand up to this religious man. I figure this answer will buy me a few more years of fence-sitting and give me time to learn what this thing called church is.

I am wrong.

Days later, Mom and I are driving in the car on a familiar road that I love for its tunnel of leafy elm trees, when she informs me, "We're on our way to your baptism!" What a confusing thing to hear. Had the bishop lied to my mother and told her I had agreed? Had she insisted he go through with the baptism despite my protests? Is this yet another one of those things that I am too young to understand?

We arrive at the chapel, and I am instructed to change into a white dress. There are two other girls about my age who are also getting baptized. There is music. There are speakers. I watch as the first girl walks down the steps into the font. She is standing in the water! Her father walks down the steps on the other side and stands behind her. He says a prayer and then dunks her under the water! Her whole body! What is happening? No one else in the room looks alarmed. She leaves the font, and I am told it is my turn. Fear swirls in my stomach and threatens to breach my throat. I recognize the man standing at the top of the stairs on the opposite side of the water as one of my mother's friends. I am encouraged to walk down the tiled steps, and the tepid water soaks my socks and the hem of my borrowed dress.

Thus began my thirty-eight-year career as a member of The Church of Jesus Christ of Latter-day Saints. Teachers and leaders reminded me many times over the years that I had to remain loyal and faithful to the Mormon Church because of the obedience I had promised at my baptism.

1984

"And how did he touch you?" I am back in the bishop's office—same office, different bishop. I have finally mustered the courage to tell him that my stepfather sexually abused me for about six months when I was eleven. As a thirteen-year-old, I am trusting and compliant. I answer all the bishop's questions, no matter how embarrassing or intrusive. I do not know what he will do with this information, but I believe presenting this sensitive material to this trusted leader will be a gateway to my healing. I believe in his power to make things better. The bishop steeples his fingers and exhales through his nose. "Because your stepfather was baptized between the time of the abuse and your reporting, there is nothing I can do. Your stepfather's sins were forgiven at his baptism. My advice is for you to get on with your life and try never to think about this again." There is no support, no talk about telling my mother, no encouragement to get therapy, no reporting to the police, no explanation about the statute of limitations. I am sent away with my burden intact and with instructions not to pursue further healing. Without warning, I find myself ushered out of the office and into the brightly lit church hallway, unable to recall how our meeting ended.

A couple of years later, my stepfather is preparing to attend the temple for the first time. I know he will have an interview with our stake president before going, to determine his worthiness. The stake president is a friend of mine, and I feel I can trust him with this secret about my abuse. I hope that somehow the issue will be addressed and that I can find some resolution to my problem. I rehearse the whole story to him, and he expresses empathy. "I'm so sorry this happened to you and that your concerns were not appropriately addressed in the past. I will handle this issue with your stepfather before he will be allowed to enter the temple."

A couple of weeks later, I am practicing the piano at home and my stepfather walks through the room and mumbles, "I'm sorry for what happened before," as he passes by. That is my apology. That is the best my stake president friend will do for me. In the following weeks, not only is my stepfather permitted to go to the temple, but he is also given a position of leadership in the congregation. He is upheld as a perfect example of the kind of man we should all aspire to be. It becomes clear to me that there will be no justice. I receive the unmistakable message that I do not matter, that I have no voice, and that predators are protected in the church and victims are silenced.

1993

"We have been visiting Valerie, like you asked. We go to her apartment every week to chat, share a positive message, pet her dog, and clean up a little, since she can't see." Valerie is a blind elderly woman in a Mormon congregation south of San Jose, California. I am a missionary serving a full-time mission for the church, and her bishop has asked my companion and me to visit members of the church in his geographical area, and to report back to him and his priesthood executive committee about them. I continue my report, "Something happened this week, though, that we're not sure you're aware of. When Valerie didn't answer her buzzer, a neighbor informed us she had passed away." I pause to determine if these men knew this about Valerie. There is awkward silence while the men exchange sheepish glances. Then the bishop bursts with the laughter he can no longer contain.

"You rang a dead woman's doorbell?" he asks with no pretense of respect for the deceased. The room erupts with levity as if I had told a joke about a rabbi, a priest, and a Mormon walking into a bar. Before I can process the meaning of this outburst, the bishop asks me about the Dawsons.

I begin hesitantly, "The Dawsons are a lovely family. They have welcomed us into their home, and we have become friends. Mr. Dawson, as you know, was excommunicated, and now that some time has passed, he has expressed interest in being rebaptized." Privately, I admire Mr. Dawson and his family for their strength and commitment to each other and to God. It does not take long for me to recognize that this room of leaders does not share my respect for this family. Winks, elbows, and chuckles take a pleasure cruise around the large oak table, as this Good Ol' Boys club whispers about the shameful things Mr. Dawson supposedly did to get kicked out of the church. I imagine cigar smoke and swirling brandy snifters accessorizing their gestures. This is the moment I announce that my companion and I will not be returning to this meeting in the future—because we do not feel comfortable sharing information with the committee.

The bishop threatens, "I'll tell your zone leaders that you're being uncooperative."

I meet the bishop's eye for a beat before responding, "Those nineteen-year-old boys don't have any authority over me." The room looks like a still life of a seven-ten split at the bowling alley. Men pause in various positions of leaning in and out of their chairs. I have their attention. I exit the room, and, true to my word, I never return.

I am three years older than most of the young men missionaries he was talking about, boys I feel are just playing at leadership. I am respectful of their male-only priesthood authority until they use it as an excuse to treat me badly.

I call my mother from our apartment, which is against the mission rules. "I want to come home. This is all bullshit!" I am angry, and desperate for compassion and understanding. My mother panics. She does not want me to return from my mission early because of the shame and embarrassment it would cause our family in front of her church friends. There is a stigma of failure for missionaries who return early. She begs me to stay.

I finish my mission and return home to look for a husband and start a family. This family goal does not come from within. It is a church mandate to pair off young people. I am not sure where I fit in the big plan, since I am gay, but I want to please my leaders and my mother.

2003

The whole wall is a window. Without curtains I feel exposed, but there are no people outside, only tall evergreens and birds of prey soaring on the invisible current of wind. Once, there was a deer, right outside the window of my solitary bedroom. I have my own bathroom with a shower, and they let Gary bring me some clothes and toiletries, but I am not allowed any belts or laces. It is a precaution they take with all the patients. The psychiatrist assigned to my case will arrive any minute. He has an offensive body odor, but I keep that to myself. I may have lost my ability to cope with reality, but I haven't lost all sense of decorum and propriety. He arrives with a nurse, and we take our seats in the padded wooden chairs. After preliminary small talk, he explains to his assistant that I am here for depression, anxiety, and possible bipolar disorder, which have been exacerbated by a traumatic event. I confirm his assessment with a nod. My brother is dead. My only sibling died in a house fire not even two months ago. Someone once told me that mourning is love with nowhere to go. His passing has left a 125-pound hole in my eleven-ounce heart. These are my darkest days, but there is more on my mind than just Steve's death.

The doctor tiptoes into more sensitive areas. "How is life at home? How is your marriage relationship?" I hesitate to answer his question. Is this the lifeline I've been waiting for? Is this my opportunity to come clean? I calculate the risk/benefit ratio on my emotional abacus. For once in my life, I need to be honest so I can heal this blistering, infected wound. I draw in a breath and look down at the floor.

"I'm attracted to women," I blurt. This is the first time I have said these words out loud, though I have been screaming them in my head for years. I pause for the anticipated lightning bolt to strike me dead. Death would be a sweet release from this pain. What I do not say is that I have suspected I was gay since I was seven years old, but the messages I got from my community were not supportive. When I was thirteen, Charles O. Howard, a man in my hometown of Bangor, Maine, was beaten to death and thrown in the river for being gay. I heard many jokes about the incident from friends and decided that I would not explore this part of myself for fear of it being true. It was not safe to be out, so I had to get as far in as possible. I have been hiding ever since. It is my understanding that homosexuals can be members of the church if they remain celibate and alone their entire lives. In the next life, they will be free from their "unclean temptation" and will be rewarded for their faithfulness with a marriage partner of the opposite gender. This doctrine is problematic for people struggling with this issue because knowing their "problem" will be solved by their death makes suicide look appealing.

"Have you told your husband? Some men think it's a real turn on," the doctor grins.

Gross.

"We're part of a strict religious community. I don't believe my husband of seven years will be happy to hear his wife is a lesbian," I reply calmly.

Church has been a huge part of my life, and it has influenced all my major life decisions. My once-in-a-lifetime patriarchal blessing told me about a future I would have with a husband who would take me to the temple to be married for eternity, and it referred many times to the children we would have within this union. My identity at church plays a key role in my sexual identity, as well. I have so many questions. I cannot make sense of the premise that a loving God created me in His own image, as I am, and then declared my nature to be unholy and impure.

On the outside I look like a content housewife and mother of two, but my secret truth is deep and dark and heavy.

I have made a mess of my life and the lives of my little family. I trusted the church's advice to get married despite my inclinations, hoping that things would work out for the best. I trusted that my urges would become correct and appropriate after marriage. I tried with all my heart and soul to make that come true; I am left bruised and bloody from the effort. And now I cannot even share this with my husband. "No, I have not told my husband," I conclude. "I don't want to lose my family."

"Oh, you're probably right," the doctor admits. "I can see why it might be risky for you to tell him." I understand that to tell Gary would mean the end of our marriage, and I do not want that. I love him and I want our children to live in a stable home. In order to avoid hurting my family, the people I love most in my life, I will need to continue as if everything were fine and not admit this secret to anyone. I have been following this course for many years, and I will have to continue for still more years into the future. The only logical option I can entertain is to try my absolute best every day to raise these innocent children to adulthood, and then when they graduate from high school, I will be free to kill myself. Gary can find someone who will love him the way he deserves to be loved. As irrational as it may seem, this scheme brings me hope. I craft the plan, sculpt it, hone it, polish it, admire it. I feel relief that there is a ripcord to pull. I have established meaning and purpose. I am determined.

2017

I turn off the car, but we are still deep in conversation. The garage flood-lights illuminate our faces, which show deep concern and love for one another. My fifteen-year-old daughter is confiding in me that she identifies as nonbinary transgender. I struggle to understand what this means—because I am unfamiliar with the complex LGBTQ lexicon. She is nervous. "Would you still love me if I was trans?"

There is no hesitation in my answer. "Bella, the only appropriate response to your question is yes—I will always love you. Thank you for trusting me with your truth."

"Thanks, Mom, I was worried about how you would react because I know you're so religious and that it could be a conflict for you."

A shell casing falls to the floor of the car. The barrel of my pistol swirls with smoke. Emotionally, I lie motionless and stunned. I have wounded myself in the process of trying to protect my kids. I have always wanted my children to feel comfortable coming to me with questions or concerns. To know that raising them in the church has contributed to the difficulty of this moment blows a hole through my middle. I have known something like this was coming for a couple of weeks. She has been feeling me out and making comments to test my reactions. I am prepared to come out to her to show my support and understanding. "I want you to know that I love and support you, and I feel safe telling you that I am a closeted lesbian."

"Really?" She is shocked. This is completely unexpected for her. Our relationship will forever be changed. We are connecting on a human level, not just in our roles as family members. We embrace and enter the house where we begin our secret-keeping from Bella's father and older brother. She comes out to them within a week, and they are surprisingly supportive. Bella assures me she will keep my confidence.

A couple weeks later, Bella, now calling themselves Rune, uploads a video to tell friends and family about their exciting news and to explain about the new name and pronouns. A youth leader in our congregation discovers the video and reports it to the church leadership. The bishop calls our family into his office to "manage expectations early." He explains that there is no such thing as nonbinary transgender. He expounds that gender is an eternal part of our nature, and it does not change or vary from set social norms. He continues, "Bella, because you have come out publicly against a church teaching, you will never be worthy to serve a mission as an official representative of the church. Your worthiness is on the same level as someone who has had multiple sexual partners, so you are no longer eligible to enter the temple of God. In addition, you must use the women's restrooms here at church, and you are only permitted to attend the classes established for females."

Rune is unflappable. I am so impressed with their poise and grace. They have written out questions for the bishop and he is selecting his words carefully and vowing to get further clarification from his superiors. Essentially, what Rune wants to know is if it is possible to be trans and still stay in the church. He offers what he thinks is encouragement. "Please be prayerful about your decision. Come back next week and let me know what Heavenly Father says about your choice."

The following Sunday we all return to the bishop's office for another round of lecture and rhetoric. When Rune reports back that they are confident God supports them on this journey, the bishop disagrees. I jump into the exchange. "So when you told them to go home and pray about it, what you were really saying was to pray until they agree with you?"

"No," he retorts defensively, but it is clear to us all that is exactly what he meant. The air in the room shifts and so does my respect for this man's authority. He warns Gary and I, "You both will need to exercise caution because you will not be worthy of your temple recommends if you believe that nonbinary gender is a real thing or that Bella was born this way." This message of exclusion cannot be from God. There is no compassion in these answers. This is not what Jesus would do. I am furious at the things the bishop has said to and about our child and I worry about long-term spiritual damage, so on our drive home from the meeting that afternoon, I tell Rune that the church is not true, like Santa Claus. Later in the day, I learn from friends that the bishop has been instructing members of the congregation that they are not permitted to call Rune by their new name or proper pronouns. He outed Rune to these people, our peers, without our knowledge or consent. Such a reckless action could potentially put Rune in danger of discrimination or even physical harm.

"I just don't think I can go back, Gary," I reason, desperately, with my husband. He knows I have been entertaining some serious doubts over the past year. I have dedicated a significant amount of time to learning about spirituality from authors of various faith traditions. What he doesn't know is that my curiosity has led me to disturbing information about church history and many inconsistencies with doctrine and policies over the years. My religious devotion to the church does not recover from these realizations. Now, the actions and words of this bishop are a new low in my church experience and yet another confirmation that this is not where I belong. This box is too small. I will not contort myself into a foreign shape to comply with these demands. I could bow to authority when the church told me I was broken, sick, and a threat to traditional family values for being gay, but I will not allow them to harm my child. I will protect Rune with every resource and faculty I possess.

My husband and older son remain faithfully devoted to the church and its leaders. Rune and I have never returned.

37

Pioneer Pattern

Alma Linda Martinez

I am not a direct descendant of the pioneers. Handcarts did not carry meager morsels and bundles of dusty family heirlooms. I have never felt the beckoning that Zion must have brought to their faithful bosoms, but on an overcast and slightly breezy July 24, I had a spark flash through me as I hugged my knees and scruffed my Corgi mutt's ears.[1] He looked up at me with a backward-crooked head cock and I felt satisfaction rising in me like steam out of a teakettle. I was creating my Zion.

His tongue dangled and then curled back into his mouth as the full-fledged doggy smile shifted to a lazy day yawn. It was my exact sentiment as I glanced down at my faded rainbow Kokopelli on my right ankle. For years I learned how to shift my body where my rainbow was covered by appendages or life accessories. Some people have nightmares of going to church in their underwear, but my nightmare was a pencil skirt and a toddler who had finally fully integrated into nursery. My exposed tattoo used to summon panic attacks. Not just the tattoo, but anything that brought attention to a life I'd sworn was behind me for good because that was the only way I believed God would love and accept me. Somehow I'd let myself believe that learning to adapt to a heteronormative society was like giving up my vodka and Pinot Noir. Hardly dear. Hardly.

I was full of satisfaction as I gazed upon the splash pad and park. There was a perfectly paired mom and dad who looked lovingly into one another's eyes while they followed their barely walking toddler. There were clusters of young mothers sitting in tiny tent cabanas and visiting. There were grandmas and grandpas playing with expansive amounts of grandchildren. Then there was me. Barefoot in a comfy Aeropostale shirt, old jeans I had transformed into cutoffs, no makeup, and a smile expressing pure contentment that I had yet to measure myself up to anyone in my vision.

I could see both my children doing life the way they both did life so contently, and because I was finally in this place where I was everything I was meant to be I didn't feel the need to begin examining how I could make them do a version of themselves I was more comfortable with. Nicholas was strolling the playground in a daydreamy state only occasionally interacting with someone as he shared the zip line with other kids. Connor was immersed in the cluster of children on the waterslide. I could see him expressing every feeling in his little body as he talked with his hands flailing in the air and his head bobbing up and down. They were both perfect, and I could finally see them perfectly.

It's taken hard work to get to a place where a public park in Utah County wouldn't make me feel like a fraud. Bringing children to prove that I had loved a man the right way, and my body had grown this evidence that I was just like everyone else. It took time to realize that using "everyone else" as a generalization left out the couples who struggled with infertility, couples who had lost their children to disease or tragedy, or men or women who never had an opportunity to marry and begin families of their own.

Living my truth feels a lot like handcart pushing some days. I've learned through experience that no one can help get my truth cart rolling. There is a space between comfort and "on to Zion" where personal inventory becomes vital. There is no magic combination or formula that I've encountered that tells me what portion of my truth is just along for the ride. The portions that have no role in shaping me, and are unnecessary for the journey. I've carried around the extra weight out of habit, knowing that it serves no purpose, but not sure how to unload it. Recently I've felt the expediency of the unloading. I've been pushing and pulling my handcart only moving it in the tiniest of increments. Knowing where I want to get versus where I am is the great motivation of unloading with efficacy and wisdom.

This is the pioneer pattern. As if there is an instinct fueling my soul. The instinct to sort and separate all of the truth I have been given, and realizing like so many others that I am missing key ingredients. The dichotomy of holding onto my deeply rooted spirituality and my innate sexuality in a meaningful way is excruciating at times. As an LDS LGBTQ individual, I've suffered tragic losses sometimes along the way. A friend or loved one who was once a part of my safety net pulls the plug on their love and involvement out of fear, misunderstanding, or because I've lived a life where pain has been a main course and I often serve it up to those around me without immediately realizing it. I'm learning to bury these losses in shallow graves. To protect what was once sacred and nourishing to my spirit. To weep or be angry for a moment, if necessary, but then to dig deeper into a collective well of strength because that kind of loss makes me hungrier to unload all of my self-destructive weaponry and get to the Zion of deeper understanding.

We are all patterned after the pioneers who sacrificed every comfort they had once known to create a future worth celebrating. Some of us sacrifice the safety of the gospel, taking our goodness into a world that will allow us to feel the love and approval that we need. Some of us sacrifice "living authentically," and choose mixed orientation marriages or celibacy. Others live courageously and embrace their truths where everyone can see them, even if it isn't accepted or celebrated. The trailblazers have my respect and admiration. We are all on the same team. We all have a role to play.

I've had moments where I can feel the Zion of my future calling to me in the walls of the temple. I've taken my burdens there to dim the light of my soul's composition to better fit into the spaces I frequent, and the message I've received so clearly time after time is that my light that shines differently than others doesn't need to be dimmed at all. I don't know how this light is meant to shine in the future because I've been so focused on nurturing it back to its original iridescence.

After years of stretching this way and that way to get the hue just right, it has been injured and repaired more times than I can count. Twenty-two years after first coming out I am finally seeing the beauty of exactly who God created me to be, and it's glorious to feel the power in that reality. For now the Zion where I have accepted my role as a single lesbian mother with a sidekick dog is alive and well. The Zion where I've released self-expectations and proposed outcomes while still believing in the truthfulness of the gospel and my place in it is still a work in progress. Most days it is 100% reality, but on bad days it is hard to not question and petition, and on the worst days it compares to walking barefoot in the snow with bloody feet.

NOTE

1. July 24 is the anniversary of Brigham Young and company arriving into the Salt Lake Valley. In the state of Utah and in the Mormon Church, it is celebrated as "Pioneer Day."

My Lord Has Come

Becca Barrus

38

"Thanks again for coming to my performance tonight! That was really cool of you."

I read and reread the message in the little blue box a couple of times as I decide how to respond. I set the phone down, take my meds, brush my teeth, wash my face, scoop out the litter box. I still don't reply because I would like to play it cool even though I am desperately not.

The next morning, I type, "I am an *incredibly* cool person so ..." adding a winky face. It's important she knows I don't take myself seriously. That I'm casual and low pressure. I'm flirting in the same offhand way I flirt with most straight girls. I know she's not interested in me. Heaven forbid I become a living manifestation of the wayward-lesbian-preying-on-the-good-and-righteous-straight-girl trope.

She is good and righteous and she is straight. And I am not straight, so I'm neither good nor righteous and I should keep my uncleanliness as contained as possible.

At no point do I physically kneel down and vocally ask God to open up a pathway between me and this girl who loves Him. Even if I had not lost the habit of praying nightly years ago, I won't embarrass myself or God by asking for something that seems so disingenuous.

But God knows my heart and I know He can feel me begging Him to let me get close to her.

There's a very specific niche of people with whom I can freely share my true feelings about God and church. Most of the time I find myself mirroring the words of whoever I'm talking to: A group of stalwart Mormons? I validate their stances, echo their sentiments. A group of understandably jaded queer post- or ex-Mormons? I validate *their* stances, echo *their* sentiments.

The things I say in either setting aren't wrong, exactly, but they're not right either, which is why I surprise myself with my honesty in texting, "But seriously, thank you for inviting me. I've been missing God in a big way recently and during the song about finding rest, He let me know He was there. So thank you for helping with that."

The vulnerability makes me feel itchy before I've even finished composing the message. Will she believe me or think I'm just saying what I think she wants to hear? Should I delete the whole thing and send a "thumbs up" emoji instead?

I hit send without revising anything. My openness is rewarded in kind.

"I know what you mean. There's a lot of chaos within and without the church and Utah and Twitter and the world and I've been feeling really discouraged by a lot of it. Sometimes it feels like too much to handle."

These are the quiet, unsure steps down a pathway neither of us seriously considered before meeting one another.

Later, for our first outside-my-place-and-hers date (because you qualify dates differently when you're queer and/or closeted and/or figuring things out in a new relationship), I find myself crying in a garden of statues depicting the life of Christ.

The date wasn't supposed to involve me crying in a garden of statues depicting the life of Christ. We had planned to eat sushi and look at Christmas lights at Thanksgiving Point, which we do. We also wind up in the Light of the World Garden. I'm not familiar with any other work by Angela Johnson—I don't even know her name until I look it up later—but the overall tone of her sculptures snag on something in my chest.

We take selfies in a bright, Christmassy gazebo and wander into a candy-cane forest where the air is filled with a surprisingly delightful scent of peppermint. I happily drink hot citrusy cider with her, unaware of the gravity of feelings that would soon overtake me.

We arrive at a statue of the woman with the issue of blood. She reaches for the hem of Christ's garment—the wings which Malachi prophesied would be filled with healing. Thinking that it would inconvenience the Savior, she doesn't want to bother Him with this request that she knows would change her life, so she stays where she is comfortable and unobtrusive. She doesn't feel she has a right to take up space—has probably been told she doesn't have a right to take up space.

Her hand stretches out in a perpetual act of hope mingled with certainty—and yet because she is bronze, because that is how she was made, she never touches it.

She is never healed.

I weep.

I understand that longing for but being distanced from sanctity. Because of the way I was made, I, too, am in a perpetual state of not quite reaching the healing wings of Jehovah. My life is good and wonderful and meaningful, but I cannot shake off my belief in crucial saving ordinances that are unavailable to me.

I stand there, long enough for my legs to complain about the cold and even though my body is urging me to get blood flowing, I can't move. Is my sexuality a condition of mortality only? Is it like unto the issue of blood? My sexuality impacts the way I interact with the world and how the world—the church—interacts with me. It's an "issue." It's a problem to solve or to ignore, to contain, to sterilize.

Until this point, my date and I were taking in displays at the same speed. I hear her boots making movements toward the next area. I should join her. Now is not the time to get sucked into religious gay ennui.

My boots stay where they are.

I stare at the statue wondering, did the woman's spiritual stewards shrug and say that her issue of blood would be fixed in the next life, and all she could do was to trust that God would finally make her whole after living a lonely, unconnected existence?

It's easy to keep at arm's length, to ignore, to contain, to sterilize issues of blood when the blood isn't yours.

"Hey." Even through the layers of shirt and sweater and coat, I feel her light touch, tentative, yet reassuring. Inquisitive, but not demanding.

"Hey." I reflexively smile at her through my tears. She smiles back, her eyebrows furrowed, questioning.

If I tell her what I'm thinking, it will ruin the date. I should shrug it off and make a flippant comment. Pivot and ask her what she's thinking. Leave this particular hem untouched.

A smattering of raindrops glint on her black leather jacket as she listens to me haltingly explain why I'm weeping. Why this sculpture causes my chest to ache. It's not a very coherent explanation. I say, "It's complex," a lot and she nods. Her eyes exude compassion. She heeds. She murmurs assurances. She gently touches my arm a few times, letting me know that she is present for this experience.

I feel witnessed, not realizing how badly I needed someone to witness me.

I grasp her hand when I'm done with my explanation and we continue moving forward.

The next statue to make me weep is one of Christ gently taking a chick into His hands. The act is so soft, His expression so tender that I'm immediately flooded with reassuring peace. I squeeze my date's hand. She squeezes mine.

I will be healed.

Healed—not made heterosexual. Made whole. Whatever that means, whatever that looks like. In this moment, I find it easy to trust that my sexuality is eternal, just like the sexuality of my straight siblings. It feels unquestionable. This experience is part of the process of perfecting me.

More so, the sparkle of her eyes across a table, the giggly minty kisses under the mistletoe, the silvery sound of her song ringing off the trees, and the crack of our laughter against the black and mostly empty gardens. Our noses burning and our thighs warming too fast in front of a fire. The tug of our hands urging each other forward are all, collectively, part of that process. They are a part of healing. Of living.

And when I die? God will see the good fruits of my life's labor—will see the outcome of those silly and serious moments—and He will not turn me away.

He will gather me like a hen gathereth her chicks and He will tell me what I already know.

That I am not broken. And that He loves me.

God Sits in My Kitchen Sometimes

Jaclyn Foster

39

God sits in my kitchen sometimes. Well, not in *my* kitchen—in the kitchen of my childhood home, a 1990s bungalow with white appliances, paisley chairs, and prairie muntins on the windows. Sometimes he's doing the dishes, sometimes he's making dinner, sometimes he's just sitting, larger than life, in thin air. But he's always perfectly at home there, as if his entire job, his natural state, is just to sit in my kitchen.

The first time it happened, I was a missionary. I felt consumed by inadequacy and was convinced I was always falling short, and one night I prayed to know if my efforts were acceptable to God. I dreamed I was two years old again, sitting at the small wooden child's table in the corner of the dining nook, busily coloring a picture while God made dinner. I picked up my masterpiece and ran eagerly into the kitchen.

"Look, Daddy, I drew a picture of us!" It was one of those scratchy, scribbled children's scrawls, with spidery overlong legs and arms poking out from a head/body. A disaster, by any objective artistic criteria.

"I love it!" God beamed. "It's beautiful." He hung it proudly on the white fridge, and I stared up at it, equally proud. It never even occurred to me to doubt his assessment, or to feel anything other than his genuine pride for me. I woke up crying.

The second time was different. Kerry and I were emailing over a blog post, and she said, "I used to think if I had a gay child, I would leave the church. Zero questions asked. But I *was* a gay child." It was a question I had been wrestling with myself: I would be able to forgive myself for leaving to protect a spouse, or a child, but myself? Why didn't my own pain matter that much? Why couldn't I validate my own need to leave?

That night, God sat in my kitchen again. I was thirteen, too old for this house, but I walked in the back door like it was how I came home from school every day. God sat, larger than life, superimposed on the kitchen sink, like he did every day. It was a normal afternoon, but my heart was pounding. I had something to tell him. "Dad, I think I'm bisexual."

God swept me straight up in his arms, bundled me into his being that thrummed with protective love. Without even hesitating, we went out to the car and drove away. The bishop called, and God told him that no, he could not speak to me, because we weren't coming back.

God left the church with me that day. In a single night, thirteen-year-old me came home from school day after day, happy and safe, knowing that who I was was okay, knowing that God would be sitting in my kitchen, happy to see me, without a word of blame or guilt for what I had become. And the worries of whether or not to leave the church, whether or not to ever come back, weren't even on my mind, because they weren't mine to handle. I came out to God, and God left the church with me.

I woke up crying.

CONTRIBUTORS

KIMBERLY ANDERSON
Kimberly Anderson is a photographer and marriage and family therapist. She is the photographer and author of the *Mama Dragon Story Project*, featuring portraits and autobiographical essays from over 135 Mormon mothers of LGBTQ children. As a marriage and family therapist, she specializes in working with LGBTQ youth and their families.

BECCA BARRUS
Becca Barrus grew up in West Jordan, Utah, as the exact middle of nine kids in a very LDS family. She is a copywriter, editor, and podcast producer for a nonprofit for 911 dispatchers and writes on the side, as well. She's currently rewriting a YA novel called *Mormon Girl* about a closeted teen girl grappling with her faith and sexuality around the Exclusion Policy. She has a BA in English from Brigham Young University.

JASPER BRENNAN
Jasper Brennan is a nonbinary, biromantic, asexual Mormon from California who just recently accepted these queer identities as a part of themself. They are an avid reader and writer (mostly of fiction) and love philosophizing about both secular and religious topics. Jasper is a recent college graduate but considers themself a lifelong student. They are continuously learning and growing, and love finding and creating meaning from the chaos and complexity around them.

CHRIS DAVIS
Once, Chris Davis was a young girl from Bangor, Maine, who wasn't brave enough to dream. She spent many unhappy years helping others achieve their goals. Finally, she grew to become the intelligent, ambitious woman she was always meant to be. She has big plans and a bright future.

AMANDA FARR

Amanda is a public health researcher who focuses on strengthening evidence-based practices through community based participatory research approaches. She has published on youth experiencing homelessness, approaches to partnerships in child welfare systems, and increasing youth voice in queer research. Raised as a Mormon in western Pennsylvania, Amanda now lives in San Diego with her partner, four children, and several dogs she does not claim as her own.

JACLYN FOSTER

Jaclyn is a historian of science and religion in American empire. She lives in Montana with her spouse and children.

CHELSEA GIBBS

Chelsea Gibbs was born and raised a member of the Church of Jesus Christ of Latter-day Saints in Westchester, New York. She began BYU-Provo in 2008 during the church's Prop 8 activism, and graduated in 2012 when the slow-growing Understanding Same Gender Attraction club was kicked off campus. She came out during her MA program at USC's Cinema School (where she learned to indulge in the occasional *Rizzoli & Isles* fanfiction), and now works as a film historian and archivist.

ARI GLASS

Ari is a nonbinary bisexual in Australia, where they are studying science and law at university. They spend their time obsessing over sports and taking care of their plants.

BEA GOODMAN

Bea is a queer designer who aims to use zier work to advocate for underrepresented voices. When the essay was written, Bea used she/her and has chosen to leave the piece unchanged despite preferring neopronouns in the present. Zie will graduate with a BA in French and communications minor in April 2021. Zie has lived in rural Utah, urban France, and Belgium, and attended university in Utah Valley, Utah.

V. H.

V. H. is a member of one of the old-guard pioneer stock Utah Mormon families. She struggled valiantly and stupidly against her flaming lesbianism until middle age, when the struggle gave way to an ongoing joyful romp. She adores her fiancée and children and wishes for all miserably mixed-orientation Mormon marriages to break up sweetly and peacefully, so the struggling humans can all love and be loved, in all the ways best for them.

METTE HARRISON

Mette Ivie Harrison holds a PhD in Germanic Languages and Literatures from Princeton University and publishes a nationally best-selling mystery series beginning with *The Bishop's Wife*. She is also an all-American triathlete, nine-time Ironman finisher, Boston-qualifying marathoner, podcaster at *The Mormon Sabbatical*, knitter, quilter, mother of five, and all-around bad-ass.

KAJA M. KANIEWSKA

Kaja is an activist and educator based in Warsaw, Poland, dividing their professional life between a fight for LGBTQ rights and promoting the cultural heritage of Polish Jews. They're currently working on a degree in philosophy. Privately, they're a *Star Trek* nerd, enjoy knitting, and love to spend church meetings hanging out with small children.

ABBY KIDD

Abby is an educator and writer who lives in Washington State with her husband, daughter, and a revolving door of other young friends who need a safe place to land.

MELISSA MALCOLM KING

Melissa Malcolm King is a freelance writer and poet who has ongoing publications with *Exponent II* and *InnerVision Magazine*. Melissa's passions include teaching Special Education, supporting LGBTQ rights, and being a voice to the marginalized through her nonprofit project B.E. S.A.F.E., serving survivors of abuse and domestic violence.

BOBBIE LEE-CORRY

Bobbie Lee-Corry grew up in Singapore and has lived in the U.S. for the last ten years. They studied documentary filmmaking at BYU and enjoy using their skills to help nonprofit causes. As the only out gay person in the Singapore Stake, Bobbie is an advocate for LGBTQ minorities, hoping to inspire Asian youth and parents, especially within the LDS faith, to rethink social norms. Bobbie has spoken at various forums and events, sharing their stories and poems about being queer and agender while being Chinese with a Mormon upbringing.

AMBER LEWIS

Amber has been married to her wonderful husband since 2017. She loves her job as a social worker, all things dogs, and Netflix. She plans on getting her MSW and working with children with trauma histories.

ALMA LINDA MARTINEZ

Alma is a loud and proud native of San Antonio, TX, with Hispanic origins. She is currently living in Pleasant Grove, UT, with her two young boys. She is an accountant by day and has found catharsis, healing, and discovery in her faith journey with writing. She is currently navigating the frontier of being openly gay and active LDS as bravely (and awkwardly) as she can. She wants to help bring understanding and empathy for LGBTQ individuals who desire to navigate their journeys in nontraditional ways.

ELIANA MASSEY

Eliana Massey is a queer Mormon feminist poet and writer. Her passion for queer spirituality has led her to be a part of the founding team of Trans Saint Stories and write essays and poetry for QMW and the Exponent's blog.

JUDITH MEHR

Judith is a well-known artist within the Mormon Church with a reputation for her portraits in particular. Her artwork was as familiar to all of us as her queerness was hidden. Her current artistic obsession is with humanity generally and human interactions more specifically. She has spent many decades painting various literal subjects such as portraits, landscapes, still lifes, and genre scenes depicting acts of everyday life in a realistic mode. Now, however, she is strongly attracted to using this realistic painting ability to speak about social issues, interpersonal relationships, the nexus of human caring, and the terror of human abuse.

REBECCA MOORE

Rebecca Moore currently works in aviation with hopes of one day becoming an astronaut. While she still considers herself culturally Mormon, she is no longer practicing.

CRISTINA MORAES

Cristina Moraes is President of Affirmation Brazil and a member of the Affirmation board of directors. Cristina has been married for twelve years to Viviane Moraes. She is a postgraduate in quality engineering and a returned missionary from the LDS Church.

BLAIRE OSTLER

Blaire Ostler is a philosopher who specializes in queer studies, and is a leading voice at the intersection of queer, Mormon, and transhumanist thought. She is an author publishing her first book, *Queer Mormon Theology*. She is a board member of the Mormon Transhumanist Association, the Christian Transhumanist Association, and Sunstone.

SARAH PACE
Sarah spends her time picking up new hobbies and waiting for a revolution. While at BYU, her passion projects were LGBTQ activism and producing short films. She currently lives in Virginia with a very small garden. Her podcast, *Moral Grounding*, looks at various fandoms through a sociological and religious lens.

JODIE PALMER
Jodie is a true blue, down to the core, fiber of her being Mormon. And, despite the potentially unpopular label, she is a true blue, down to the core, fiber of her being lesbian. She courts the seemingly impossible marriage between the two, while also navigating a decade-plus mixed-orientation marriage (MOM) with her husband. The ménage à trois of faith, sexuality, and chosen partner has at times vacillated between ecstasy and suicidality, yet she keeps pursuing the elusive "and."

FRANK PELLETT
Frank is a software developer for the LDS Church and believes strongly in the church and the gospel.

TAYLOR PETREY
Taylor Petrey is an American scholar of religion and editor of *Dialogue: A Journal of Mormon Thought* since 2019. He is an associate professor at Kalamazoo College. In 2016–17, he was a visiting associate professor at Harvard Divinity School and research associate at the Women's Studies in Religion Program. He is author of *Tabernacles of Clay: Gender and Sexuality in Modern Mormonism* (Chapel Hill: UNC Press, 2020).

KERRY SPENCER PRAY
Kerry got her PhD from the University of Wales and taught writing at BYU for 15 years. She now teaches writing at Stevenson University and lives in Maryland with her wife and children.

KEL PURCILL
Kel Purcill is a queer Australian woman about to begin her PhD in Creative Writing. Kel has had fiction and nonfiction published in Australia and internationally. Twitter: @SelwynsSanity

AISLING "ASH" ROWAN
Ash Rowan is an autistic artist, general enthusiast, and creator of GEM (Gender-Expansive Mormon) Stories—formerly Trans Saint Stories. Describing themself as "liminally Mormon" and a spiritual wanderer, Ash strives to emulate the devoted discipleship and radically inclusive kindness

of Fred Rogers, while seeking truth and light wherever it may be found. Ash currently lives with their spouse and sprogs in the valleys of Utah.

NAJI HASKA RUNS THROUGH
Naji is a federally enrolled member of the Assiniboine tribe in Fort Peck, Montana. They are genderqueer, bisexual, two-spirit, and are a semiactive member of the church who graduated high school in May 2020.

IRVING DIEGO SANTOS
Irving Diego is a twenty-four-year-old trans man who loves movies, series, football, and recently discovered a new passion for analog photography. He lives in the state of Tocantins, in Brazil, and wants to do gastronomy or film school someday.

JENN LEE SMITH
Jenn is a Taiwan-born Asian American, queer filmmaker who shares stories of underrepresented people.

JENNY SMITH
Jenny is a mom, pharmacy tech, and recovering addict. After spending forty-two years as a devout Mormon, she now considers herself Mormon-adjacent. She lives in Utah with her two fabulous sons and two very peculiar cats.

MIRANDA YBARRA
Miranda is your average young adult, on the search for the perfect clam chowder and a passionate advocate for queer rights after death. Miranda loves long road trips through the National Parks and reading any book they can get their hands on. Miranda lives in Washington State with their partner and a fluffy black cat named Zip.